LATIMER'S SERMONS

HUGH LATIMER.

From the drawing by J. Childe.

SELECTED SERMONS OF

HUGH LATIMER

BISHOP AND MARTYR

With an Introduction and Notes
by the

Rev. A. R. BUCKLAND, M.A.

Morning Preacher at the Foundling Hospital

PHILADELPHIA

THE UNION PRESS

1122 CHESTNUT STREET

1904

CONTENTS

HUGH LATIMER

Born at Thurcaston, *c.* 1490.

Graduated at Cambridge, 1510.

Preached the Sermons on the Card, 1529.

Summoned before Convocation, 1532.

Bishop of Worcester, 1535.

Resigned his See, 1539.

Sent to the Tower, 1553.

Burnt at Oxford, 1555.

INTRODUCTION

LATIMER AS A PREACHER

'I HAVE an ear for other preachers, but I have a heart for Latimer,' said Sir John Cheke, the learned tutor of Edward VI. Even a selection of Latimer's sermons may show why, amongst the great preachers of the Reformation era, his influence was pre-eminent. Such popular strength as lay behind the movement was very largely due to the work of preachers, and amongst them not one was more efficient than Hugh Latimer. Whether he preached before the Court, or before Convocation, or at his own University of Cambridge, or in a country district, he seems with equal certainty to have compelled attention.

The simple exposition of Holy Scripture which so often supplies the substance of Latimer's sermon came to hearers of the period with a freshness it could not have for the same kind of audiences to-day. But at Latimer's lips such an exposition was never dull and never unpractical. He worked into it plain statements of Reformation doctrine, and, as occasion served, he dealt with the teaching and practices of the unreformed clergy with unsparing frankness.

His Cambridge contemporary, Thomas Becon, one of Cranmer's chaplains, exultingly catalogues the subjects he heard Latimer treat in this fashion. In truth, Latimer was never more himself than when he was denouncing non-preaching dignitaries, or ' Purgatory pick-purse,' or some gross imposture like the Blood of Hales. But he did not limit his censure to the ways and teaching of the unreformed Church. The irreligious world was scarcely less often the object of his scorn and his appeals. No preacher has ever more boldly impeached London for its sins of the flesh, or has ever spoken more fearlessly of the great and powerful.

These qualities would have themselves sufficed to win attention for Latimer ; but to them must be added his style as a speaker. No one was ever less of the polished orator, although he sometimes broke out into passages of natural eloquence. But Latimer was ever the plain man, who spoke out of the fulness of his heart. And to a way of delivering his mind frankly he added the use of a gift of homely wit and humour, which must have inspired his opponents with dread. Sometimes he coined a phrase that stuck, sometimes a sentence not to be forgotten, as when he spoke of Purgatory as ' the fiery furnace that hath burned away so many of our pence.' Occasionally he threw in a telling anecdote. Witness the reason given by 'a gentlewoman of London' for going to church. 'Marry,' said she, 'I am going to St Thomas of Acres to the sermon; I could not sleep all last night, and I am now going thither; I never failed of a good nap there.' Now and then he fell into reminiscence, as when he recalled the circumstances of his boyhood, or again when he spoke of a place where the church he had intended to preach in was empty, for 'the parish' were 'gone abroad to gather for Robin Hood.' One thing, in truth, is obvious; Latimer could never have been a dull preacher. Moreover, people trusted the man, 'so conformable,' as Becon tells us, 'was his life to his doctrine.'

Modern circumstances forbid us to feel that Latimer's scathing denunciations of the characteristic doctrines and practices of the Church of Rome can be deemed out of date. But, even if they were, his sermons would still allow us to say with Strype (*Ecc. Mem.* III. i. 376):—— 'Did ever there any man flourish, I say not in England only, but in any nation in the world, after the Apostles, who preached the Gospel more sincerely, purely, and honestly, than Hugh Latimer?' Judged by influence upon their hearers and upon the history of their time, no man's sermons could more justly be called 'great.' Rightly has Latimer been described[1] by one of his

[1] Sermon at the consecration of the Bishop Latimer Memorial Church, Handsworth, Birmingham, July 1904.

successors in the See of Worcester (Dr Gore), as 'a great preacher of righteousness, a great and vigorous lover of God's people, a prince of Christian Socialists, and one of the best English pulpit orators.'

From a sentence in a sermon preached at Stamford it would appear that some of Latimer's sermons were published in his life-time. Thomas Soame collected the sermons before King Edward and some others, which appeared in 1549. In 1562, John Day, with the assistance of Augustine Bernher, Latimer's Swiss servant, issued a larger collection. Other editions appeared in 1571, 1572, 1584, 1607, and 1635. The best modern edition of the sermons is that edited for the Parker Society by Professor Corrie, the text of which I have mainly followed, and some of the notes of which I have quoted.

The present selection of the sermons has been made with the view of exhibiting fairly the characteristics of the preacher and the development of his doctrinal views. They are arranged in chronological order.

A. R. BUCKLAND.

August 1904.

SERMONS ON THE CARD [1]

I

St John i. 19.—'This is the record of John, when the Jews sent Priests and Levites from Jerusalem to ask him, Who art thou?'

Tu quis es?   Which words are as much to say in English, 'Who art thou?' These be the words of the Pharisees, which were sent by the Jews unto St John Baptist in the wilderness, to have knowledge of him who he was: which words they spake unto him of an evil intent, thinking

---

[1] Preached in St Edward's Church, Cambridge, on Dec. 19, 1529. Card-playing was general in the celebration of Christmas. Latimer sought to turn the custom to good account. His bold attack upon certain ecclesiastical customs was deeply resented. Buckenham, Prior of the Dominicans, was put up to answer Latimer. He met Latimer's Christmas cards with a sermon on Christmas dice. Latimer was ready with his reply, which Buckenham went to hear. Latimer took advantage of the presence of his adversary in dealing with the use of metaphor in Holy Scripture. 'Every speech,' said he, 'hath its metaphors, so common and vulgar to all men, that the very painters do paint them on walls and in houses. As for example' [and here he looked straight at Buckenham], 'when they paint a fox preaching out of a friar's cowl, none is so mad as to take this to be a fox that preacheth, but know well enough the meaning of the matter which is to point out unto us what hypocrisy, craft, and dissimulation lie hid many times in these friars' cowls, willing us thereby to beware of them.'

that he would have taken on him to be Christ, and so they would have had him done with their good wills, because they knew that he was more carnal, and given to their laws, than Christ indeed should be, as they perceived by their old prophecies; and also, because they marvelled much of his great doctrine, preaching, and baptizing, they were in doubt whether he was Christ or not: wherefore they said unto him, 'Who art thou?' Then answered St John, and confessed that he was not Christ.

Now here is to be noted the great and prudent answer of St John Baptist unto the Pharisees, that when they required of him who he was, he would not directly answer of himself what he was himself, but he said he was not Christ: by the which saying he thought to put the Jews and Pharisees out of their false opinion and belief towards him, in that they would have had him to exercise the office of Christ; and so declared further unto them of Christ, saying, 'He is in the midst of you and amongst you, whom ye know not, whose latchet of His shoe I am not worthy to unloose, or undo.'

By this you may perceive that St John spake much in the laud and praise of Christ his Master, professing himself to be in no wise like unto Him. So likewise it shall be necessary unto all men and women of this world, not to ascribe unto themselves any goodness of themselves, but all unto our Lord God, as shall appear hereafter, when this question aforesaid, 'Who art thou?' shall be moved unto them; not as the Pharisees did unto St John, of an evil purpose, but of a good and simple mind, as may appear hereafter.

Now then, according to the preacher's mind, let every man and woman, of a good and simple mind, contrary to the Pharisees' intent, ask this question, 'Who art thou?' This question must be moved to themselves, what they be of themselves, on this fashion: 'What art thou of thy only and natural generation between father and mother, when thou camest into this world? What substance, what virtue, what goodness art thou of, by thyself'? Which question if thou rehearse oftentimes unto thyself, thou shalt well perceive and understand how thou shalt make answer unto it; which must be made on this wise: I am of myself, and by myself, coming from my natural father and mother, the child of the ire and indignation of God, the true inheritor of hell, a lump of sin, and working nothing of myself but all towards hell, except I have better help of another than I have of myself. Now we may see in what state we enter into this world, that we be of ourselves the true and just inheritors of hell, the children of the ire and indignation of Christ, working all towards hell, whereby we deserve of ourselves perpetual damnation, by the right judgment of God, and the true claim of ourselves; which unthrifty state that we be born unto is come unto us for our own deserts, as proveth well this example following:

Let it be admitted for the probation of this, that it might please the king's grace now being to accept into his favour a mean man, of a simple degree and birth, not born to any possession; whom the king's grace favoureth, not because this person hath of himself deserved any such favour, but that the king casteth this favour unto him of his own mere motion and fantasy: and for because the king's grace will more declare his favour unto him, he giveth unto this said man a thousand pounds in lands, to him and his heirs, on this condition, that he shall take upon him to be the chief captain and defender of his town of Calais,[1] and to be true and faithful to him in the custody of the same, against the Frenchmen especially, above all other enemies.

This man taketh on him this charge, promising his fidelity thereunto. It chanceth in process of time, that by the singular acquaintance and frequent familiarity of this captain with the Frenchmen, these Frenchmen give unto the said captain of Calais a great sum of money, so that he will but be content and agreeable that they may enter into the said town of Calais by force of arms; and so thereby possess the same unto the crown of France. Upon this agreement the Frenchmen

[1] Calais, taken by Edward III. in 1346, was at this time still in English hands. It was lost under Queen Mary in 1558.

do invade the said town of Calais, alonely by the negligence of this captain.

Now the king's grace, hearing of this invasion, cometh with a great puissance to defend this his said town, and so by good policy of war overcometh the said Frenchmen, and entereth again into his said town of Calais. Then he, being desirous to know how these enemies of his came thither, maketh profound search and inquiry by whom this treason was conspired. By this search it was known and found his own captain to be the very author and the beginner of the betraying of it. The king, seeing the great infidelity of this person, dischargeth this man of his office, and taketh from him and from his heirs this thousand pounds of possessions. Think you not that the king doth use justice unto him, and all his posterity and heirs? Yes, truly: the said captain cannot deny himself but that he had true justice, considering how unfaithfully he behaved him to his prince, contrary to his own fidelity and promise. So likewise it was of our first father Adam. He had given unto him the spirit of science and knowledge, to work all goodness therewith: this said spirit was not given alonely unto him, but unto all his heirs and posterity. He had also delivered him the town of Calais, that is to say, paradise in earth, the most strong and fairest town in the world, to be in his custody. He nevertheless, by the instigation of these Frenchmen, that is to say, the temptation of the fiend, did obey unto their desire; and so he brake his promise and fidelity, the commandment of the everlasting King his master, in eating of the apple by him inhibited.

Now then the King, seeing this great treason in His captain, deposed him of the thousand pounds of possessions, that is to say, from everlasting life in glory, and all his heirs and posterity : for likewise as he had the spirit of science and knowledge, for him and his heirs ; so in like manner, when he lost the same, his heirs also lost it by him and in him. So now this example proveth, that by our father Adam we had once in him the very inheritance of everlasting joy ; and by him, and in him, again we lost the same.

The heirs of the captain of Calais could not by any manner of claim ask of the king the right and title of their father in the thousand pounds of possessions, by reason the king might answer and say unto them, that although their father deserved not of himself to enjoy so great possessions, yet he deserved by himself to lose them, and greater, committing so high treason, as he did, against his prince's commandments ; whereby he had no wrong to lose his title, but was unworthy to have the same, and had therein true justice. Let not you think, which be his heirs, that if he had justice to lose his possessions, you have wrong to lose the same.

In the same manner it may be answered unto all men and women now being, that if our father Adam had true justice to be excluded from his possession of everlasting glory in paradise, let us not think the contrary that be his heirs, but that we have no wrong in losing also the same ; yea, we have true justice and right. Then in what miserable estate we be, that of the right and just title of our own deserts have lost the everlasting joy, and claim of ourselves to be true inheritors of hell ! For he that committeth deadly sin willingly bindeth himself to be inheritor of everlasting pain : and so did our forefather Adam willingly eat of the apple forbidden. Wherefore he was cast out of the everlasting joy in paradise into this corrupt world, amongst all vileness, whereby of himself he was not worthy to do any thing laudable or pleasant to God, evermore bound to corrupt affections and beastly appetites, transformed into the most uncleanest and variablest nature that was made under heaven ; of whose seed and disposition all the world is lineally descended, insomuch that this evil nature is so fused and shed from one into another, that at this day there is no man nor woman living, that can of themselves wash away this abominable vileness : and so we must needs grant of ourselves to be in like displeasure unto God, as our forefather Adam was. By reason hereof, as I said, we be of ourselves the very children of the

B

indignation and vengeance of God, the true inheritors of hell, and working all towards hell :
which is the answer to this question, made to every
man and woman, by themselves, ' Who art thou ? '

And now, the world standing in this damnable
state, cometh in the occasion of the incarnation
of Christ.   The Father in heaven, perceiving the
frail nature of man, that he, by himself and of
himself, could do nothing for himself, by His
prudent wisdom sent down the second person in
Trinity, His Son Jesus Christ, to declare unto man
His pleasure and commandment : and so, at the
Father's will, Christ took on Him human nature,
being willing to deliver man out of this miserable
way, and was content to suffer cruel passion in
shedding His blood for all mankind ; and so left
behind for our safeguard laws and ordinances, to
keep us always in the right path unto everlasting
life, as the evangelists, the sacraments, the commandments, and so forth : which if we do keep
and observe according to our profession, we shall
answer better unto this question, ' Who art thou ? '
than we did before.   For before thou didst enter
into the sacrament of baptism, thou wert but a
natural man, a natural woman ; as I might say, a
man, a woman : but after thou takest on thee
Christ's religion, thou hast a longer name ; for
then thou art a Christian man, a Christian woman.
Now then, seeing thou art a Christian man, what
shall be thy answer of this question, ' Who art thou?'

The answer of this question is, when I ask it unto myself, I must say that I am a Christian man, a Christian woman, the child of everlasting joy, through the merits of the bitter passion of Christ. This is a joyful answer. Here we may see how much we be bound and in danger unto God, that hath revived us from death to life, and saved us that were damned : which great benefit we cannot well consider, unless we do remember what we were of ourselves before we meddled with Him or His laws ; and the more we know our feeble nature, and set less by it, the more we shall conceive and know in our hearts what God hath done for us ; and the more we know what God hath done for us, the less we shall set by ourselves, and the more we shall love and please God : so that in no condition we shall either know ourselves or God, except we do utterly confess ourselves to be mere vileness and corruption. Well, now it is come unto this point, that we be Christian men, Christian women, I pray you what doth Christ require of a Christian man, or of a Christian woman ? Christ requireth nothing else of a Christian man or woman, but that they will observe His rule : for likewise as he is a good Augustine friar that keepeth well St Augustine's rule, so is he a good Christian man that keepeth well Christ's rule.

Now then, what is Christ's rule ? Christ's rule consisteth in many things, as in the commandments, and the works of mercy, and so forth. And for because I cannot declare Christ's rule unto you at one time, as it ought to be done, I will apply myself according to your custom at this time of Christmas : I will, as I said, declare unto you Christ's rule, but that shall be in Christ's cards. And whereas you are wont to celebrate Christmas in playing at cards, I intend, by God's grace, to deal unto you Christ's cards, wherein you shall perceive Christ's rule. The game that we will play at shall be called the triumph,[1] which, if it be well played at, he that dealeth shall win ; the players shall likewise win ; and the standers and lookers upon shall do the same ; insomuch that there is no man that is willing to play at this triumph with these cards, but they shall be all winners, and no losers.

Let therefore every Christian man and woman play at these cards, that they may have and obtain the triumph : you must mark also that the triumph must apply to fetch home unto him all the other cards, whatsoever suit they be of. Now then, take ye this first card, which must appear and be shewed unto you as followeth : you have heard what was spoken to men of the old law, 'Thou shalt not kill ; whosoever shall kill shall be in danger of judgment : but I say unto you' of the new law, saith Christ, 'that whosoever is angry with his neighbour, shall be in danger of

---

[1] A card game of the period.

judgment; and whosoever shall say unto his neighbour, " Raca," that is to say, brainless,' or any other like word of rebuking, ' shall be in danger of council ; and whosoever shall say unto his neighbour, " Fool," shall be in danger of hell-fire.' This card was made and spoken by Christ, as appeareth in the fifth chapter of St Matthew.

Now it must be noted, that whosoever shall play with this card, must first, before they play with it, know the strength and virtue of the same : wherefore you must well note and mark terms, how they be spoken, and to what purpose. Let us therefore read it once or twice, that we may be the better acquainted with it.

Now behold and see, this card is divided into four parts : the first part is one of the commandments that was given unto Moses in the old law, before the coming of Christ ; which commandment we of the new law be bound to observe and keep, and it is one of our commandments. The other three parts spoken by Christ be nothing else but expositions unto the first part of this commandment : for in very effect all these four parts be but one commandment, that is to say, ' Thou shalt not kill.' Yet nevertheless, the last three parts do shew unto thee how many ways thou mayest kill thy neighbour contrary to this commandment : yet, for all Christ's exposition in the three last parts of this card, the terms be not open enough to thee that dost read and hear them spoken. No doubt, the Jews understood Christ well enough, when He spake to them these three last sentences; for He spake unto them in their own natural terms and tongue. Wherefore, seeing that these terms were natural terms of the Jews, it shall be necessary to expound them, and compare them unto some like terms of our natural speech, that we in like manner may understand Christ as well as the Jews did.

We will begin first with the first part of this card, and then after, with the other three parts. You must therefore understand that the Jews and the Pharisees of the old law, to whom this first part, this commandment, 'Thou shalt not kill,' was spoken, thought it sufficient and enough for their discharge, not to kill with any manner of material weapon, as sword, dagger, or with any such weapon; and they thought it no great fault whatsoever they said or did by their neighbours, so that they did not harm or meddle with their corporal bodies: which was a false opinion in them, as prove well the three last other sentences following the first part of this card.

Now, as touching the three other sentences, you must note and take heed, what difference is between these three manner of offences: to be angry with your neighbour; to call your neighbour 'brainless,' or any such word of disdain; or to call your neighbour 'fool.' Whether these three manner of offences be of themselves more grievous one than the other, it is to be opened unto you.   Truly, as they be of themselves divers offences, so they kill diversly, one more than the other ; as you shall perceive by the first of these three, and so forth.   A man which conceiveth against his neighbour or brother ire or wrath in his mind, by some manner of occasion given unto him, although he be angry in his mind against his said neighbour, he will peradventure express his ire by no manner of sign, either in word or deed : yet nevertheless he offendeth against God, and breaketh this commandment in killing his own soul ; and is therefore 'in danger of judgment.'

Now, to the second part of these three : That man that is moved with ire against his neighbour, and in his ire calleth his neighbour 'brainless,' or some other like word of displeasure ; as a man might say in a fury, 'I shall handle thee well enough ;' which words and countenances do more represent and declare ire to be in this man, than in him that was but angry, and spake no manner of word nor shewed any countenance to declare his ire.   Wherefore as he that so declareth his ire, either by word or countenance, offendeth more against God, so he both killeth his own soul, and doth that in him is to kill his neighbour's soul in moving him unto ire, wherein he is faulty himself ; and so this man is 'in danger of council.'

Now to the third offence, and last of these three: That man that calleth his neighbour 'fool,' doth more declare his angry mind toward him, than he that called his neighbour but 'brainless,' or any such words moving ire: for to call a man 'fool,' that word representeth more envy in a man, than 'brainless' doth. Wherefore he doth most offend, because he doth most earnestly with such words express his ire, and so he is 'in danger of hell-fire.'

Wherefore you may understand now, these three parts of this card be three offences, and that one is more grievous to God than the other, and that one killeth more the soul of man than the other.

Now peradventure there be some that will marvel, that Christ did not declare this commandment by some greater faults of ire, than by these which seem but small faults, as to be angry and speak nothing of it, to declare it and to call a man 'brainless,' and to call his neighbour 'fool:' truly these be the smallest and the least faults that belong to ire, or to killing in ire. Therefore beware how you offend in any kind of ire: seeing that the smallest be damnable to offend in, see that you offend not in the greatest. For Christ thought, if He might bring you from the smallest manner of faults, and give you warning to avoid the least, He reckoned you would not offend in the greatest and worst, as to call your neighbour thief, drab, and so forth, into more blasphemous names ; which offences must needs have punishment in hell, considering how that Christ hath appointed these three small faults to have three degrees of punishment in hell, as appeareth by these three terms, judgment, council, and hell-fire. These three terms do signify nothing else but three divers punishments in hell, according to the offences. Judgment is less in degree than council, therefore it signifieth a lesser pain in hell, and it is ordained for him that is angry in his mind with his neighbour, and doth express his malice neither by word nor countenance. Council is a less degree in hell than hell-fire, and is a greater degree in hell than judgment ; and it is ordained for him that calleth his neighbour ' brainless,' or any such word, that declareth his ire and malice : wherefore it is more pain than judgment. Hell-fire is more pain in hell, than council or judgment, and it is ordained for him that calleth his neighbour ' fool,' by reason that in calling his neighbour ' fool,' he declareth more his malice, in that it is an earnest word of ire : wherefore hell-fire is appointed for it ; that is, the most pain of the three punishments.

Now you have heard, that to these divers offences of ire and killing be appointed punishments according to their degrees : for look as the offence is, so shall the pain be : if the offence be great, the pain shall be according ; if it be less, there shall be less pain for it.   I would not now

that you should think, because that here are but
three degrees of punishment spoken of, that there
be no more in hell. No doubt Christ spake of no
more here but of these three degrees of punishment, thinking they were sufficient, enough for
example, whereby we might understand, that there
be as divers and many pains as there be offences :
and so by these three offences, and these three
punishments, all other offences and punishments
may be compared with another. Yet I would
satisfy your minds further in these three terms, of
'judgment, council, and hell-fire.' Whereas you
might say, What was the cause that Christ
declared more the pains of hell by these terms,
than by any other terms ? I told you afore that
He knew well to whom He spake them. These
terms were natural and well known amongst the
Jews and the Pharisees : wherefore Christ taught
them with their own terms, to the intent they
might understand the better His doctrine. And
these terms may be likened unto three terms
which we have common and usual amongst us,
that is to say, the sessions of inquirance, the
sessions of deliverance, and the execution-day.
Sessions of inquirance is like unto judgment ; for
when sessions of inquiry is, then the judges cause
twelve men to give verdict of the felon's crime,
whereby he shall be judged to be indicted :
sessions of deliverance is much like council ; for
at sessions of deliverance the judges go among

themselves to council, to determine sentence against the felon : execution-day is to be compared unto hell-fire ; for the Jews had amongst themselves a place of execution, named 'hell-fire :'[1] and surely when a man goeth to his death, it is the greatest pain in this world. Wherefore you may see that there are degrees in these our terms, as there be in those terms.

These evil-disposed affections and sensualities in us are always contrary to the rule of our salvation. What shall we do now or imagine, to thrust down these Turks and to subdue them ? It is a great ignominy and shame for a Christian man to be bond and subject unto a Turk : nay, it shall not be so ; we will first cast a trump in their way, and play with them at cards, who shall have the better. Let us play therefore on this fashion with this card. Whensoever it shall happen the foul passions and Turks to rise in our stomachs against our brother or neighbour, either for unkind words, injuries, or wrongs, which they have done unto us, contrary unto our mind ; straightways let us call unto our remembrance, and speak this question unto ourselves, 'Who art thou ?' The answer is, 'I am a Christian man.'

Then further we must say to ourselves, 'What requireth Christ of a Christian man ?' Now turn

[1] 2 Kings xxiii. 10, Isaiah xxx. 33, Jer. vii. 31, 32.

up your trump, your heart (hearts is trump, as I said before), and cast your trump, your heart, on this card; and upon this card you shall learn what Christ requireth of a Christian man,—not to be angry, be moved to ire against his neighbour, in mind, countenance, nor other ways, by word or deed. Then take up this card with your heart, and lay them together: that done, you have won the game of the Turk, whereby you have defaced and overcome him by true and lawful play. But, alas for pity! the Rhodes [1] are won and overcome by these false Turks; the strong castle Faith is decayed, so that I fear it is almost impossible to win it again.

The great occasion of the loss of this Rhodes is by reason that Christian men do so daily kill their own nation, that the very true number of Christianity is decayed; which murder and killing one of another is increased specially two ways, to the utter undoing of Christendom, that is to say, by example and silence. By example, as thus: when the father, the mother, the lord, the lady, the master, the dame, be themselves overcome with these Turks, they be continual swearers, avouterers,[2] disposers to malice, never in patience, and so forth in all other vices: think you not, when the father,

[1] The Island of Rhodes was captured from the Knights Hospitallers by the Turks in 1523, so that the event was fresh in the minds of Latimer's hearers.

[2] Adulterers. 'Or avouterer or ellis a paramour.' Chaucer, *C. T.*

the mother, the master, the dame, be disposed
unto vice or impatience, but that their children
and servants shall incline and be disposed to the
same ? No doubt, as the child shall take disposition natural of the father and mother, so shall
the servants apply unto the vices of their masters
and dames : if the heads be false in their faculties
and crafts, it is no marvel if the children, servants
and apprentices do joy therein. This is a great
and shameful manner of killing Christian men,
that the fathers, the mothers, the masters, and the
dames, shall not alonely kill themselves, but all
theirs, and all that belongeth unto them : and so
this way is a great number of Christian lineage
murdered and spoiled.

The second manner of killing is silence. By
silence also is a great number of Christian men
slain ; which is on this fashion : although that the
father and mother, master and dame, of themselves
be well disposed to live according to the law of
God, yet they may kill their children and servants
in suffering them to do evil before their own
faces, and do not use due correction according
unto their offences. The master seeth his servant
or apprentice take more of his neighbour than the
king's laws, or the order of his faculty, doth admit
him ; or that he suffereth him to take more of
his neighbour than he himself would be content
to pay, if he were in like condition : thus doing,
I say, such men kill willingly their children and

servants, and shall go to hell for so doing ; but also their fathers and mothers, masters and dames, shall bear them company for so suffering them.

Wherefore I exhort all true Christian men and women to give good example unto your children and servants, and suffer not them by silence to offend. Every man must be in his own house, according to St Augustine's mind, a bishop, not alonely giving good ensample, but teaching according to it, rebuking and punishing vice ; not suffering your children and servants to forget the laws of God. You ought to see them have their belief, to know the commandments of God, to keep their holy-days, not to lose their time in idleness : if they do so, you shall all suffer pain for it, if God be true of His saying, as there is no doubt thereof. And so you may perceive that there be many a one that breaketh this card, ' Thou shalt not kill,' and playeth therewith often-time at the blind trump, whereby they be no winners, but great losers. But who be those now-a-days that can clear themselves of these manifest murders used to their children and servants ? I think not the contrary, but that many have these two ways slain their own children unto their damnation ; unless the great mercy of God were ready to help them when they repent there-for.

Wherefore, considering that we be so prone and ready to continue in sin, let us cast down our-

selves with Mary Magdalene ; and the more we
bow down with her toward Christ's feet, the more
we shall be afraid to rise again in sin ; and the
more we know and submit ourselves, the more we
shall be forgiven ; and the less we know and
submit ourselves, the less we shall be forgiven ;
as appeareth by this example following :

Christ, when He was in this world amongst the
Jews and Pharisees, there was a great Pharisee
whose name was Simon :[1] this Pharisee desired
Christ on a time to dine with him, thinking in
himself that he was able and worthy to give
Christ a dinner. Christ refused not his dinner,
but came unto him. In time of their dinner it
chanced there came into the house a great and
a common sinner named Mary Magdalene. As
soon as she perceived Christ, she cast herself
down, and called unto her remembrance what she
was of herself, and how greatly she had offended
God ; whereby she conceived in Christ great love,
and so came near unto Him, and washed His feet
with bitter tears, and shed upon His head precious
ointment, thinking that by Him she should be
delivered from her sins. This great and proud
Pharisee, seeing that Christ did accept her oblation
in the best part, had great indignation against this
woman, and said to himself, ' If this man Christ
were a holy prophet, as He is taken for, He
would not suffer this sinner to come so nigh

[1] Luke vii. 36-50.

Him.' Christ, understanding the naughty mind
of this Pharisee, said unto him, ' Simon, I have
somewhat to say unto thee.' ' Say what You
please,' quod the Pharisee. Then said Christ, ' I
pray thee, tell Me this : If there be a man to
whom is owing twenty pound by one, and forty
by another, this man to whom this money is
owing, perceiving these two men be not able to
pay him, he forgiveth them both : which of these
two debtors ought to love this man most ? ' The
Pharisee said, ' That man ought to love him best,
that had most forgiven him.' ' Likewise,' said
Christ, ' it is by this woman : she hath loved Me
most, therefore most is forgiven her ; she hath
known her sins most, whereby she hath most
loved Me. And thou hast least loved Me, because
thou hast least known thy sins : therefore, because
thou hast least known thine offences, thou art
least forgiven.' So this proud Pharisee had an
answer to delay his pride. And think you not,
but that there be amongst us a great number of
these proud Pharisees, which think themselves
worthy to bid Christ to dinner ; which will perk,
and presume to sit by Christ in the church, and
have a disdain of this poor woman Magdalene,
their poor neighbour, with a high, disdainous, and
solemn countenance ? And being always desirous
to climb highest in the church, reckoning themselves more worthy to sit there than another, I
fear me poor Magdalene under the board, and in

the belfry, hath more forgiven of Christ than they have : for it is like that those Pharisees do less know themselves and their offences, whereby they less love God, and so they be less forgiven.

I would to God we would follow this example, and be like unto Magdalene.   I doubt not but we be all Magdalenes in falling into sin and in offending : but we be not again Magdalenes in knowing ourselves, and in rising from sin.   If we be the true Magdalenes, we should be as willing to forsake our sin and rise from sin, as we were willing to commit sin and to continue in it ; and we then should know ourselves best, and make more perfect answer than ever we did unto this question, 'Who art thou?' to the which we might answer, that we be true Christian men and women : and then, I say, you should understand, and know how you ought to play at this card, 'Thou shalt not kill,' without any interruption of your deadly enemies the Turks ; and so triumph at the last, by winning everlasting life in glory. Amen.

c

SERMONS ON THE CARD

II

St John i. 19.—'This is the record of John,' etc.

NOW you have heard what is meant by this first card, and how you ought to play with it, I purpose again to deal unto you another card, almost of the same suit ; for they be of so nigh affinity, that one cannot be well played without the other. The first card declared, that you should not kill, which might be done divers ways ; as being angry with your neighbour, in mind, in countenance, in word, or deed : it declared also, how you should subdue the passions of ire, and so clear evermore yourselves from them. And whereas this first card doth kill in you these stubborn Turks of ire ; this second card will not only they should be mortified in you, but that you yourselves shall cause them to be likewise mortified in your neighbour, if that your said neighbour hath been through your occasion moved unto ire, either in countenance, word, or deed. Now let us hear, therefore, the tenor of this card : ' When thou makest thine oblation at Mine altar, and

24

there dost remember that thy neighbour hath any thing against thee, lay down there thy oblation, and go first and reconcile thy neighbour, and then come and offer thy oblation.'[1]

This card was spoken by Christ, as testifieth St Matthew in his fifth chapter, against all such as do presume to come unto the church to make oblation unto God either by prayer, or any other deed of charity, not having their neighbours reconciled. Reconciling is as much to say as to restore thy neighbour unto charity, which by thy words or deeds is moved against thee : then, if so be it that thou hast spoken to or by thy neighbour, whereby he is moved to ire or wrath, thou must lay down thy oblation. Oblations be prayers, alms-deeds, or any work of charity : these be all called oblations to God. Lay down, therefore, thine oblation ; begin to do none of these foresaid works before thou goest unto thy neighbour, and confess thy fault unto him ; declaring thy mind, that if thou hast offended him, thou art glad and willing to make him amends, as far forth as thy words and substance will extend, requiring him not to take it at the worst : thou art sorry in thy mind, that thou shouldest be occasion of his offending.

'What manner of card is this?' will some say : 'Why, what have I to do with my neighbour's or brother's malice?' As Cain said, 'Have I the

---

[1] Matt. v. 23, 24.

keeping of my brother? or shall I answer for him and for his faults? This were no reason—— As for myself, I thank God I owe no man malice nor displeasure: if others owe me any, at their own peril be it. Let every man answer for himself!' Nay, sir, not so, as you may understand by this card; for it saith, 'If thy neighbour hath any thing, any malice against thee, through thine occasion, lay even down (saith Christ) thine oblation: pray not to Me; do no good deeds for Me; but go first unto thy neighbour, and bring him again unto My flock, which hath forsaken the same through thy naughty words, mocks, scorns, or disdainous countenance, and so forth; and then come and offer thine oblation; then do thy devotion; then do thy alms-deeds; then pray, if thou wilt have Me hear thee.'

'O good Lord! this is a hard reckoning, that I must go and seek him out that is offended with me, before I pray or do any good deed. I cannot go unto him. Peradventure he is a hundred miles from me, beyond the seas; or else I cannot tell where: if he were here nigh, I would with all my heart go unto him.' This is a lawful excuse before God on this fashion, that thou wouldest in thy heart be glad to reconcile thy neighbour, if he were present; and that thou thinkest in thy heart, whensoever thou shalt meet with him, to go unto him, and require him charitably to forgive thee; and so never intend to come from him, until the time that you both depart one from the other true brethren in Christ.

Yet, peradventure, there be some in the world that be so devilish and so hard-hearted, that they will not apply in any condition unto charity. For all that, do what lieth in thee, by all charitable means to bring him to unity. If he will in no wise apply thereunto, thou mayest be sorrowful in thy heart, that by thine occasion that man or woman continueth in such a damnable state. This notwithstanding, if thou do the best that lieth in thee to reconcile him, according to some doctors' mind, thou art discharged towards God. Nevertheless St Augustine doubteth in this case, whether thy oblations, prayers, or good deeds, shall avail thee before God, or no, until thy neighbour come again to good state, whom thou hast brought out of the way. Doth this noble doctor doubt therein? What aileth us to be so bold, and count it but a small fault, or none, to bring our neighbour out of patience for every trifle that standeth not with our mind? You may see what a grievous thing this is, to bring another man out of patience, that peradventure you cannot bring in again with all the goods that you have: for surely, after the opinion of great wise men, friendship once broken will be never well made whole again. Wherefore you shall hear what Christ saith unto such persons.

Saith Christ, ' I came down into this world, and so took on Me bitter passion for man's sake, by the merits whereof I intended to make unity and peace in mankind, to make man brother unto Me, and so to expel the dominion of Satan, the devil, which worketh nothing else but dissension : and yet now there be a great number of you, that have professed My name, and say you be Christian men, which do rebel against My purpose and mind.   I go about to make My fold : you go about to break the same, and kill My flock.' ' How darest thou,' saith Christ, ' presume to come unto My altar, unto My church, or into My presence, to make oblation unto Me, that takest on thee to spoil My lambs ?   I go about like a good shepherd to gather them together ; and thou dost the contrary, ever more ready to divide and lose them.   Who made thee so bold to meddle with my silly beasts, which I bought so dearly with My precious blood ?   I warn thee out of My sight, come not in My presence : I refuse thee and all thy words, except thou go and bring home again My lambs which thou hast lost. Wherefore, if thou thyself intend to be one of Mine, lay even down by and by thine oblation, and come no further toward Mine altar ; but go and seek them without any questions, as it becometh a true and faithful servant.'

A true and faithful servant, whensoever his master commandeth him to do anything, he

maketh no stops nor questions, but goeth forth
with a good mind : and it is not unlike he, con-
tinuing in such a good mind and will, shall well
overcome all dangers and stops, whatsoever betide
him in his journey, and bring to pass effectually
his master's will and pleasure. On the contrary,
a slothful servant, when his master commandeth
him to do any thing, by and by he will ask
questions, 'Where?' 'When?' 'Which way?'
and so forth ; and so he putteth every thing in
doubt, that although both his errand and way be
never so plain, yet by his untoward and slothful
behaviour his master's commandment is either
undone quite, or else so done that it shall stand
to no good purpose. Go now forth with the
good servant, and ask no such questions, and put
no doubts. Be not ashamed to do thy Master's
and Lord's will and commandment. Go, as I
said, unto thy neighbour that is offended by thee,
and reconcile him (as is afore said) whom thou
hast lost by thy unkind words, by thy scorns,
mocks, and other disdainous words and behaviours ;
and be not nice to ask of him the cause why he
is displeased with thee : require of him charitably
to remit ; and cease not till you both depart, one
from the other, true brethren in Christ.

Do not, like the slothful servant, thy master's
message with cautels [1] and doubts ; come not to
thy neighbour whom thou hast offended, and give

[1] Tricks or cunning ways. *Cf.* Shaks. *Ham.* i. 3.

him a pennyworth of ale, or a banquet, and so make him a fair countenance, thinking that by thy drink or dinner he will shew thee like countenance. I grant you may both laugh and make good cheer, and yet there may remain a bag of rusty malice, twenty years old, in thy neighbour's bosom. When he departeth from thee with a good countenance, thou thinkest all is well then. But now, I tell thee, it is worse than it was, for by such cloaked charity, where thou dost offend before Christ but once, thou hast offended twice herein : for now thou goest about to give Christ a mock, if He would take it of thee. Thou thinkest to blind thy Master Christ's commandment. Beware, do not so, for at length He will overmatch thee, and take thee tardy whatsoever thou be ; and so, as I said, it should be better for thee not to do His message on this fashion, for it will stand thee in no purpose.

'What ?' some will say, 'I am sure he loveth me well enough : he speaketh fair to my face.' Yet for all that thou mayest be deceived. It proveth not true love in a man, to speak fair. If he love thee with his mind and heart, he loveth thee with his eyes, with his tongue, with his feet, with his hands and his body ; for all these parts of a man's body be obedient to the will and mind. He loveth thee with his eyes, that looketh cheerfully on thee, when thou meetest with him, and is glad to see thee prosper and do well. He loveth thee with his tongue, that speaketh well by thee behind thy back, or giveth thee good counsel. He loveth thee with his feet, that is willing to go to help thee out of trouble and business. He loveth thee with his hands, that will help thee in time of necessity, by giving some alms-deeds, or with any other occupation of the hand. He loveth thee with his body, that will labour with his body, or put his body in danger to do good for thee, or to deliver thee from adversity : and so forth, with the other members of his body. And if thy neighbour will do according to these sayings, then thou mayest think that he loveth thee well ; and thou, in like wise, oughtest to declare and open thy love unto thy neighbour in like fashion, or else you be bound one to reconcile the other, till this perfect love be engendered amongst you.

It may fortune thou wilt say, 'I am content to do the best for my neighbour that I can, saving myself harmless.' I promise thee, Christ will not hear this excuse ; for He Himself suffered harm for our sakes, and for our salvation was put to extreme death. I wis, if it had pleased Him, He might have saved us and never felt pain ; but in suffering pains and death He did give us example, and teach us how we should do one for another, as He did for us all ; for, as He saith Himself, 'he that will be Mine, let him deny himself, and follow Me, in bearing

My cross and suffering My pains.' Wherefore we must needs suffer pain with Christ to do our neighbour good, as well with the body and all his members, as with heart and mind.

Now I trust you wot what your card meaneth : let us see how that we can play with the same. Whensoever it shall happen you to go and make your oblation unto God, ask of yourselves this question, 'Who art thou ?' The answer, as you know, is, 'I am a Christian man.' Then you must again ask unto yourself, What Christ requireth of a Christian man? By and by cast down your trump, your heart, and look first of one card, then of another. The first card telleth thee, thou shalt not kill, thou shalt not be angry, thou shalt not be out of patience. This done, thou shalt look if there be any more cards to take up ; and if thou look well, thou shalt see another card of the same suit, wherein thou shalt know that thou art bound to reconcile thy neighbour. Then cast thy trump upon them both, and gather them all three together, and do according to the virtue of thy cards ; and surely thou shalt not lose. Thou shalt first kill the great Turks, and discomfort and thrust them down. Thou shalt again fetch home Christ's sheep that thou hast lost ; whereby thou mayest go both patiently and with a quiet mind unto the Church, and make thy oblation unto God ; and then, without doubt, He will hear thee.

But yet Christ will not accept our oblation (although we be in patience, and have reconciled our neighbour), if that our oblation be made of another man's substance; but it must be our own. See therefore that thou hast gotten thy goods according to the laws of God and of thy prince. For if thou gettest thy goods by polling and extortion, or by any other unlawful ways, then, if thou offer a thousand pound of it, it will stand thee in no good effect; for it is not thine. In this point a great number of executors do offend; for when they be made rich by other men's goods, then they will take upon them to build churches, to give ornaments to God and His altar, to gild saints, and to do many good works therewith; but it shall be all in their own name, and for their own glory. Wherefore, saith Christ, they have in this world their reward; and so their oblations be not their own, nor be they acceptable before God.

Another way God will refuse thy voluntary oblation, as thus: if so be it that thou hast gotten never so truly thy goods, according both to the laws of God and man, and hast with the same goods not relieved thy poor neighbour, when thou hast seen him hungry, thirsty, and naked, he will not take thy oblation when thou shalt offer the same, because he will say unto thee, 'When I was hungry, thou gavest me no meat; when I was thirsty, thou gavest no drink; and when I was naked, thou didst not clothe me. Wherefore I will not take thy oblation, because it is none of thine. I left it thee to relieve thy poor neighbours, and thou hast not therein done according unto this my commandment, *Misericordiam volo, et non sacrificium ;* I had rather have mercy done, than sacrifice or oblation. Wherefore until thou dost the one more than the other, I will not accept thine oblation.'

Evermore bestow the greatest part of thy goods in works of mercy, and the less part in voluntary works. Voluntary works be called all manner of offering in the church, except your four offering-days,[1] and your tithes : setting up candles, gilding and painting, building of churches, giving of ornaments, going on pilgrimages, making of highways, and such other, be called voluntary works ; which works be of themselves marvellous good, and convenient to be done. Necessary works, and works of mercy, are called the commandments, the four offering-days,[1] your tithes, and such other that belong to the commandments ; and works of mercy consist in relieving and visiting thy poor neighbours. Now then, if men be so foolish of themselves, that they will bestow the most part of

---

[1] The usual offering-days were at Christmas, Easter, Whitsuntide, and the Feast of the dedication of the parish church. But by injunctions put forth by Henry VIII. in the year 1538, 'the Feasts of the Nativity of our Lord, of Easter-day, of the Nativity of St John the Baptist, and of St Michael the Archangel, were to be 'taken for the four general offering-days.' Strype, *Annals*, I. xlii. (*Corrie*).

their goods in voluntary works, which they be not
bound to keep, but willingly and by their devotion ;
and leave the necessary works undone, which they
are bound to do ; they and all their voluntary
works are like to go unto everlasting damnation.
And I promise you, if you build a hundred churches,
give as much as you can make to gilding of
saints, and honouring of the church ; and if
thou go as many pilgrimages as thy body can
well suffer, and offer as great candles as oaks ;
if thou leave the works of mercy and the commandments undone, these works shall nothing
avail thee.

No doubt the voluntary works be good and
ought to be done ; but yet they must be so done,
that by their occasion the necessary works and the
works of mercy be not decayed and forgotten.
If you will build a glorious church unto God, see
first yourselves to be in charity with your neighbours, and suffer not them to be offended by your
works. Then, when ye come into your parish
church, you bring with you the holy temple of
God ; as St Paul saith, ' You yourselves be the
very holy temples of God:' and Christ saith by His
prophet, ' In you will I rest, and intend to make
My mansion and abiding-place.'[1]   Again, if you
list to gild and paint Christ in your churches, and
honour Him in vestments, see that before your
eyes the poor people die not for lack of meat,

[1] Ezek. xxxvii. 26, 27.

drink, and clothing.   Then do you deck the very
true temple of God, and honour Him in rich
vestures that will never be worn, and so forth use
yourselves according unto the commandments :
and then, finally, set up your candles, and they
will report what a glorious light remaineth in your
hearts ; for it is not fitting to see a dead man light
candles.   Then, I say, go your pilgrimages, build
your material churches, do all your voluntary
works ; and they will then represent you unto
God, and testify with you, that you have provided
Him a glorious place in your hearts.   But beware,
I say again, that you do not run so far in your
voluntary works, that ye do quite forget your
necessary works of mercy, which you are bound
to keep : you must have ever a good respect unto
the best and worthiest works toward God to be
done first and with more efficacy, and the other to
be done secondarily.

Thus if you do, with the other that I have
spoken of before, ye may come according to the
tenor of your cards, and offer your oblations and
prayers to our Lord Jesus Christ, Who will both
hear and accept them to your everlasting joy and
glory : to the which He brings us, and all those
whom He suffered death for.   Amen.

THE SERMON BEFORE CONVOCATION: MORNING [1]

St Luke xvi. 8.—' *For the children of this world . . . light.*'

BRETHREN, ye be come together this day, as far as I perceive, to hear of great and weighty matters. Ye be come together to entreat of things that most appertain to the commonwealth. This being thus, ye look, I am assured, to hear of me, which am commanded to make as a preface this exhortation (albeit I am unlearned and far unworthy), such things as shall be much meet for this your assembly. I therefore, not only very desirous to obey the commandment of our Primate, but also right greatly coveting to serve and satisfy all your expectation, lo, briefly, and as plainly as I can, will speak of matters both worthy to be heard in your congregation, and

[1] This sermon, delivered in Latin, was preached before the Convocation of Canterbury on June 9, 1536. Latimer had been made Bishop of Worcester in the preceding year. It was the first meeting of Convocation after the break with Rome, and Latimer's boldness in denouncing practices which many of his hearers still favoured, amply justified his choice by Archbishop Cranmer for the office. Four years before this, in 1532, Cranmer had himself been summoned before Convocation to answer for his opinions (see Demaus's *Hugh Latimer*, pp. 145 *et seq.*, ed. 1904).

also of such as best shall become mine office in
this place.   That I may do this the more commodiously, I have taken that notable sentence in
which our Lord was not afraid to pronounce
'the children of this world to be much more
prudent and politic than the children of light
in their generation.'   Neither will I be afraid,
trusting that He will aid and guide me to use this
sentence, as a good ground and foundation of all
such things as hereafter I shall speak of.

Now, I suppose that you see right well, being
men of such learning, for what purpose the Lord
said this, and that ye have no need to be holpen
with any part of my labour in this thing.   But
yet, if ye will pardon me, I will wade somewhat
deeper in this matter, and as nigh as I can, fetch
it from the first original beginning.   For undoubtedly, ye may much marvel at this saying,
if ye well ponder both what is said, and who
saith it.   Define me first these three things :
what prudence is ; what the world ; what light ;
and who be the children of the world ; who of
the light : see what they signify in scripture.   I
marvel if by and by ye all agree, that the children
of the world should be wiser than the children of
the light.   To come somewhat nigher the matter,
thus the Lord beginneth :

There was a certain rich man that had a steward,
which was accused unto him that he had

dissipated and wasted his goods. This rich man called his steward to him and said, What is this that I hear of thee? Come, make me an account of thy stewardship; thou mayest no longer bear this office.[1]

Brethren, because these words are so spoken in a parable, and are so wrapped in wrinkles, that yet they seem to have a face and a similitude of a thing done indeed, and like an history, I think it much profitable to tarry somewhat in them. And though we may perchance find in our hearts to believe all that is there spoken to be true; yet I doubt whether we may abide it, that these words of Christ do pertain unto us, and admonish us of our duty, which do and live after such sort, as though Christ, when He spake any thing, had, as the time served Him, served His turn, and not regarded the time that came after Him, neither provided for us, or any matters of ours; as some of the philosophers thought, which said, that God walked up and down in heaven, and thinketh never a deal of our affairs. But, my good brethren, err not you so; stick not you to such your imaginations. For if ye inwardly behold these words, if ye diligently roll them in your minds, and after explicate and open them, ye shall see our time much touched in these mysteries. Ye shall perceive that God

[1] Luke xvi. 1, 2.

D

by this example shaketh us by the noses and pulleth us by the ears. Ye shall perceive very plain, that God setteth before our eyes in this similitude what we ought most to flee, and what we ought soonest to follow. For Luke saith, ' The Lord spake these words to His disciples.' Wherefore let it be out of all doubt that He spake them to us, which even as we will be counted the successors and vicars of Christ's disciples, so we be, if we be good dispensers and do our duty. He said these things partly to us, which spake them partly of Himself. For He is that rich man, which not only had, but hath, and shall have evermore, I say not one, but many stewards, even to the end of the world.

He is man, seeing that He is God and man. He is rich, not only in mercy but in all kind of riches ; for it is He that giveth to us all things abundantly. It is He of Whose hand we received both our lives, and other things necessary for the conservation of the same. What man hath any thing, I pray you, but he hath received it of His plentifulness ? To be short, it is He that ' openeth His hand, and filleth all beasts with His blessing,' and giveth unto us in most ample wise His benediction. Neither His treasure can be spent, how much soever He lash out ; how much soever we take of Him, His treasure tarrieth still, ever taken, never spent.

He is also the good man of the house ; the

church is His household, which ought with all
diligence to be fed with His word and His sacraments. These be His goods most precious, the
dispensation and administration whereof He would
bishops and curates should have. Which thing
St Paul affirmeth, saying, 'Let men esteem us as
the ministers of Christ, and dispensers of God's
mysteries.' But, I pray you, what is to be looked
for in a dispenser? This surely, 'that he be
found faithful,' and that he truly dispense, and
lay out the goods of the Lord; that he give meat
in time; give it, I say, and not sell it; meat I
say, and not poison. For the one doth intoxi-
cate and slay the eater, the other feedeth and
nourisheth him. Finally, let him not slack and
defer the doing of his office, but let him do his duty
when time is, and need requireth it. This is also
to be looked for, that he be one whom God hath
called and put in office, and not one that cometh
uncalled, unsent for; not one that of himself pre-
sumeth to take honour upon him. And surely, if all
this that I say be required in a good minister, it
is much lighter to require them all in every one,
than to find one any where that hath them all.
Who is a true and faithful steward? He is true,
he is faithful, that coineth no new money, but
taketh it ready coined of the good man of the
house; and neither changeth it, nor clippeth it,
after it is taken to him to spend, but spendeth
even the self-same that he had of his Lord, and

spendeth it as his Lord's commandment is;
neither to his own vantage uttering it, nor as the
lewd servant did, hiding it in the ground.

Brethren, if a faithful steward ought to do as I
have said, I pray you, ponder and examine this
well, whether our bishops and abbots, prelates
and curates, have been hitherto faithful stewards
or no. Ponder, whether yet many of them be
as they should be or no. Go ye to, tell me now
as your conscience leadeth you (I will let pass to
speak of many other), was there not some, that
despising the money of the Lord, as copper and
not current, either coined new themselves, or else
uttered abroad newly coined of other; some time
either adulterating the word of God, or else mingling
it (as taverners do, which brew and utter the evil
and good both in one pot), sometime in the stead
of God's word blowing out the dreams of men?
while they thus preached to the people the
redemption that cometh by Christ's death to
serve only them that died before His coming,
that were in the time of the Old Testament;
and that now since redemption and forgiveness
of sins purchased by money, and devised by
men, is of efficacy, and not redemption purchased
by Christ: (they have a wonderful pretty example to persuade this thing, of a certain married
woman, which, when her husband was in purgatory, in that fiery furnace that hath burned away
so many of our pence, paid her husband's ransom,

and so of duty claimed him to be set at liberty :)
while they thus preached to the people, that dead
images (which at the first, as I think, were set up,
only to represent things absent) not only ought
to be covered with gold, but also ought of all
faithful and Christian people (yea, in this scarce-
ness and penury of all things), to be clad with silk
garments, and those also laden with precious gems
and jewels ; and that beside all this, they are to
be lighted with wax candles, both within the
church and without the church, yea, and at noon
days ; as who should say, here no cost can be too
great ; whereas in the meantime we see Christ's
faithful and lively images, bought with no less
price than with His most precious blood (alas,
alas !) to be an hungred, a-thirst, a-cold, and to lie
in darkness, wrapped in all wretchedness, yea, to
lie there till death take away their miseries : while
they preached these will-works, that come but of
our own devotion, although they be not so
necessary as the works of mercy, and the precepts
of God, yet they said, and in the pulpit, that
will-works were more principal, more excellent,
and (plainly to utter what they mean) more
acceptable to God than works of mercy ; as
though now man's inventions and fancies could
please God better than God's precepts, or strange
things better than his own : while they thus
preached that more fruit, more devotion cometh
of the beholding of an image, though it be but a

Pater-noster while, than is gotten by reading and contemplation in scripture, though ye read and contemplate therein seven years' space : finally, while they preached thus, souls tormented in purgatory to have most need of our help, and that they can have no aid, but of us in this world : of the which two, if the one be not false, yet at the least it is ambiguous, uncertain, doubtful, and therefore rashly and arrogantly with such boldness affirmed in the audience of the people ; the other, by all men's opinions, is manifestly false : I let pass to speak of much other such like counterfeit doctrine, which had been blasted and blown out by some for the space of three hours together. Be these the Christian and divine mysteries, and not rather the dreams of men ? Be these the faithful dispensers of God's mysteries, and not rather false dissipators of them? whom God never put in office, but rather the devil set them over a miserable family, over an house miserably ordered and entreated. Happy were the people if such preached seldom.

And yet it is a wonder to see these, in their generation, to be much more prudent and politic than the faithful ministers are in their generation ; while they go about more prudently to stablish men's dreams, than these do to hold up God's commandments.

Thus it cometh to pass that works lucrative, will-works, men's fancies reign ; but Christian works, necessary works, fruitful works, be trodden under the foot. Thus the evil is much better set out by evil men, than the good by good men; because the evil be more wise than be the good in their generation. These be the false stewards, whom all good and faithful men every day accuse unto the rich master of the household, not without great heaviness, that they waste his goods; whom he also one day will call to him, and say to them as he did to his steward, when he said, 'What is this that I hear of thee?' Here God partly wondereth at our ingratitude and perfidy, partly chideth us for them; and being both full of wonder and ready to chide, asketh us, 'What is this that I hear of you?' As though He should say unto us: 'All good men in all places complain of you, accuse your avarice, your exactions, your tyranny. They have required in you a long season, and yet require, diligence and sincerity. I commanded you, that with all industry and labour ye should feed My sheep: ye earnestly feed yourselves from day to day, wallowing in delights and idleness. I commanded you to teach My commandments, and not your fancies; and that ye should seek My glory and My vantage; you teach your own traditions, and seek your own glory and profit. You preach very seldom; and when ye do preach, do nothing but cumber them that preach truly, as much as lieth in you; that it were much better such were not to preach at all, than so perniciously to preach. Oh, what hear I of you? You, that ought to be My preachers, what other thing do you, than apply all your study hither, to bring all My preachers to envy, shame, contempt? Yea, more than this, ye pull them into perils, into prisons, and, as much as in you lieth, to cruel deaths. To be short, I would that Christian people should hear My doctrine, and at their convenient leisure read it also, as many as would: your care is not that all men may hear it, but all your care is, that no lay man do read it: surely, being afraid lest they by the reading should understand it, and understanding, learn to rebuke our slothfulness. This is your generation, this is your dispensation, this is your wisdom. In this generation, in this dispensation, you be most politic, most witty. These be the things that I hear of your demeanour. I wished to hear better report of you. Have ye thus deceived Me? or have ye rather deceived yourselves? Where I had but one house, that is to say, the church, and this so dearly beloved of Me, that for the love of her I put Myself forth to be slain, and to shed My blood; this church at My departure I committed unto your charge, to be fed, to be nourished, and to be made much of. My pleasure was ye should occupy My place; My desire was ye should have borne like love to this church, like fatherly affection, as I did: I made you My vicars, yea, in matters of most importance.

' For thus I taught openly : " He that should hear you, should hear Me ; he that should despise you, should despise me."[1]   I gave you also keys, not earthly keys, but heavenly.[2]   I left My goods that I have evermore most highly esteemed, that is, My word and sacraments, to be dispensed of you.   These benefits I gave you, and do you give Me these thanks ?   Can you find in your hearts thus to abuse My goodness, My benignity, My gentleness ?   Have you thus deceived Me ?   No, no, ye have not deceived Me, but yourselves.   My gifts and benefits toward you shall be to your greater damnation.   Because you have contemned the lenity and clemency of the master of the house, ye have right well deserved to abide the rigour and severity of the judge.   Come forth then, let us see an account of your stewardship.   An horrible and fearful sentence : Ye may have no longer My goods in your hands.   A voice to weep at, and to make men tremble ! '

You see, brethren, you see, what evil the evil stewards must come to.   Your labour is paid for, if ye can so take heed, that no such sentence be spoken to you ; nay, we must all take heed lest these threatenings one day take place in us.   But lest the length of my sermon offend you too sore, I will leave the rest of the parable and take me to the handling of the end of it ; that is, I will

[1] Luke x. 16.   [2] Matt. xvi. 19.

declare unto you how the children of this world
be more witty, crafty, and subtle, than are the
children of the light in their generation. Which
sentence would God it lay in my poor tongue to
explicate with such light of words, that I might
seem rather to have painted it before your eyes,
than to have spoken it; and that you might
rather seem to see the thing, than to hear it!
But I confess plainly this thing to be far above
my power. Therefore this being only left to me,
I wish for that I have not, and am sorry that
that is not in me which I would so gladly have,
that is, power so to handle the thing that I have
in hand, that all that I say may turn to the glory
of God, your soul's health, and the edifying of
Christ's body. Wherefore I pray you all to pray
with me unto God, and that in your petition you
desire, that these two things He vouchsafe to
grant us, first, a mouth for me to speak rightly;
next, ears for you, that in hearing me ye may
take profit at my hand: and that this may come
to effect, you shall desire Him, unto whom our
Master Christ bade we should pray, saying even
the same prayer that He Himself did institute.
Wherein ye shall pray for our most gracious
sovereign lord the king, chief and supreme head
of the church of England under Christ,[1] and for
the most excellent, gracious, and virtuous lady

[1] The Royal Supremacy, declared by the Act of Parliament, 26
Henry VIII., c. 11, completed the break with Rome.

queen Jane,[1] his most lawful wife, and for all his, whether they be of the clergy or laity, whether they be of the nobility, or else other his grace's subjects, not forgetting those that being departed out of this transitory life, and now sleep in the sleep of peace, and rest from their labours in quietness and in peaceable sleep, faithfully, lovingly, and patiently looking for that that they clearly shall see when God shall be so pleased. For all these, and for grace necessary, ye shall say unto God God's prayer, *Paternoster.*

[1] Jane Seymour, the third wife of Henry VIII. She died in the following year, 1537.

THE SERMON BEFORE CONVOCATION :
AFTERNOON

St Luke xvi. 8.—'The children of this world . . . light.'

CHRIST in this saying touched the sloth and sluggishness of His, and did not allow the fraud and subtlety of others ; neither was glad that it was indeed as He had said, but complained rather that it should be so : as many men speak many things, not that they ought to be so, but that they are wont to be so. Nay, this grieved Christ, that the children of this world should be of more policy than the children of light ; which thing was true in Christ's time, and now in our time is most true. Who is so blind but he seeth this clearly ; except perchance there be any that cannot discern the children of the world from the children of light ? The children of the world conceive and bring forth more prudently ; and things conceived and brought forth they nourish and conserve with much more policy than do the children of light. Which thing is as sorrowful to be said, as it seemeth absurd to be heard.

When ye hear the children of the world, you understand the world as a father. For the world

is father of many children, not by the first creation
and work, but by imitation of love. He is not
only a father, but also the son of another father.
If ye know once his father, by and by ye shall
know his children. For he that hath the devil to
his father, must needs have devilish children. The
devil is not only taken for father, but also for
prince of the world, that is, of worldly folk. It is
either all one thing, or else not much different, to
say, children of the world, and children of the
devil ; according to that that Christ said to the
Jews, 'Ye are of your father the devil' ; [1] where
as undoubtedly He spake to children of this world.
Now seeing the devil is both author and ruler of
the darkness, in the which the children of this
world walk, or, to say better, wander ; they mortally
hate both the light, and also the children of light.
And hereof it cometh, that the children of light
never, or very seldom, lack persecution in this
world, unto which the children of the world, that
is, of the devil, bringeth them. And there is no
man but he seeth, that these use much more
policy in procuring the hurt and damage of the
good, than those in defending themselves. Therefore, brethren, gather you the disposition and study
of the children by the disposition and study of the
fathers. Ye know this is a proverb much used :
'An evil crow, an evil egg.' Then the children
of this world that are known to have so evil a

[1] John viii. 44.

father, the world, so evil a grandfather, the devil,
cannot choose but be evil. Surely the first head
of their ancestry was the deceitful serpent the devil,
a monster monstrous above all monsters. I cannot
wholly express him, I wot not what to call him,
but a certain thing altogether made of the hatred
of God, of mistrust in God, of lyings, deceits, per-
juries, discords, manslaughters ; and, to say at one
word, a thing concrete, heaped up and made of all
kind of mischief. But what the devil mean I to
go about to describe particularly the devil's nature,
when no reason, no power of man's mind can
comprehend it? This alonely I can say grossly,
and as in a sum, of the which all we (our hurt is
the more) have experience, the devil to be a stink-
ing sentine [1] of all vices ; a foul filthy channel of
all mischiefs ; and that this world, his son, even a
child meet to have such a parent, is not much
unlike his father.

Then, this devil being such one as can never
be unlike himself ; lo, of Envy, his well beloved
Leman, he begat the World, and after left it with
Discord at nurse ; which World, after that it came
to man's state, had of many concubines many sons.
He was so fecund a father, and had gotten so
many children of Lady Pride, Dame Gluttony,
Mistress Avarice, Lady Lechery, and of Dame
Subtlety, that now hard and scant ye may find

---

[1] Sentine, *sentina*, the lowest part in the hold of a ship, where
the bilge-water collected.

any corner, any kind of life, where many of his
children be not. In court, in cowls, in cloisters,
in rochets, be they never so white ; yea, where
shall ye not find them ? Howbeit, they that be
secular and laymen are not by and by children
of the world ; nor they children of light that are
called spiritual, and of the clergy. No, no ; as ye
may find among the laity many children of light,
so among the clergy (how much soever we arro-
gate these holy titles unto us, and think them
only attributed to us, *Vos estis lux mundi, peculium
Christi, etc.* 'Ye are the light of the world,[1] the
chosen people of Christ, a kingly priesthood, an
holy nation, and such other'[2]), ye shall find many
children of the world ; because in all places the
world getteth many children.

Among the lay people the world ceaseth not
to bring to pass, that as they be called worldly
so they are worldly indeed ; driven headlong by
worldly desires : insomuch that they might right
well seem to have taken as well the manners as
the name of their father. In the clergy, the world
also hath learned a way to make of men spiritual,
worldlings ; yea, and there also to form worldly
children, where with great pretence of holiness,
and crafty colour of religion, they utterly desire
to hide and cloak the name of the world, as though
they were ashamed of their father ; which do
execrate and detest the world (being neverthe-

---

[1] Matt. v. 14. [2] 1 Pet. ii. 9.

less their father) in words and outward signs, but in heart and work they coll[1] and kiss him, and in all their lives declare themselves to be his babes; insomuch that in all worldly points they far pass and surmount those that they call seculars, lay-men, men of the world. The child so diligently followeth the steps of his father, is never destitute of the aid of his grandfather.

These be our holy, holy men, that say they are dead to the world, when no men be more lively in worldly things than some of them be. But let them be in profession and name most farthest from the world, most alienate from it; yea so far, that they may seem to have no occupying, no kindred, no affinity, nothing to do with it: yet in their life and deeds they show themselves no bastards, but right begotten children of the world; as that which the world long sithens had by his dear wife Dame Hypocrisy, and since hath brought them up and multiplied to more than a good many; increased them too much, albeit they swear by all he-saints and she-saints too, that they know not their father, nor mother, neither the world, nor hypocrisy; as indeed they can semble and dissemble all things; which thing they might learn wonderful well of their parents. I speak not of all religious men, but of those that the world hath fast knit at his girdle, even in the

---

[1] To embrace, to clasp around the neck. "Colled me aboute the nekke."—*Piers Plowman.*

midst of their religion, that is, of many and more than many. For I fear, lest in all orders of men the better, I must say the greater part of them be out of order, and children of the world. Many of these might seem ingrate and unkind children, that will no better acknowledge and recognise their parents in words and outward pretence, but abrenounce and cast them off, as though they hated them as dogs and serpents. Howbeit they, in this wise, are most grateful to their parents, because they be most like them, so lively representing them in countenance and conditions, that their parents seem in them to be young again, forasmuch as they ever say one thing and think another. They shew themselves to be as sober, as temperate, as Curius [1] the Roman was, and live every day as though all their life was a shroving time.[2] They be like their parents, I say, inasmuch as they, in following them, seem and make men believe they hate them. Thus grandfather Devil, father World, and mother Hypocrisy, have brought them up. Thus good obedient sons have borne away their parents' commandments; neither these be solitary, how religious, how mocking, how monking, I would say, soever they be.

O ye will lay this to my charge, that *monachus* and *solitarius* signifieth all one. I grant this to

[1] M. Curius Dentatus, the Roman Consul, whose simplicity and frugality became proverbial.

[2] That is a time for confession and absolution; especially the time when people were shriven preparatory to Lent.

E

be so, yet these be so solitary that they be not alone, but accompanied with great flocks of fraternities. And I marvel if there be not a great sort of bishops and prelates, that are brethren germain unto these; and as a great sort, so even as right born, and world's children by as good title as they. But because I cannot speak of all, when I say prelates, I understand bishops, abbots, priors, archdeacons, deans, and other of such sort, that are now called to this convocation, as I see, to entreat here of nothing but of such matters as both appertain to the glory of Christ, and to the wealth of the people of England. Which thing I pray God they do as earnestly as they ought to do. But it is to be feared lest, as light hath many her children here, so the world hath sent some of his whelps hither: amongst the which I know there can be no concord nor unity, albeit they be in one place, in one congregation. I know there can be no agreement between these two, as long as they have minds so unlike, and so contrary affections, judgments so utterly diverse in all points. But if the children of this world be either more in number, or more prudent than the children of light, what then availeth us to have this convocation? Had it not been better we had not been called together at all? For as the children of this world be evil, so they breed and bring forth things evil; and yet there be more of them in all places, or at the least they be more politic than the children of light in their generation.

And here I speak of the generation whereby they do engender, and not of that whereby they are engendered, because it should be too long to entreat how the children of light are engendered, and how they come in at the door ; and how the children of the world be engendered, and come in another way. Howbeit, I think all you that be here were not engendered after one generation, neither that ye all came by your promotions after one manner : God grant that ye, engendered worldly, do not engender worldly : and as now I much pass not how ye were engendered, or by what means ye were promoted to those dignities that ye now occupy, so it be honest, good and profitable, that ye in this your consultation shall do and engender.

The end of your convocation shall shew what ye have done ; the fruit that shall come of your consultation shall shew what generation ye be of. For what have ye done hitherto, I pray you, these seven years and more ? What have ye engendered ? What have ye brought forth ? What fruit is come of your long and great assembly ? What one thing that the people of England hath been the better of a hair ; or you yourselves, either more accepted before God, or better discharged toward the people committed unto your cure ? For that the people is better

learned and taught now, than they were in the
time past, to whether of these ought we to attribute
it, to your industry, or to the providence of God,
and the foreseeing of the king's grace ? [1] Ought
we to thank you, or the king's highness ? Whether
stirred other first, you the king, that he might
preach, or he you by his letters, that ye should
preach oftener ? Is it unknown, think you,
how both ye and your curates were, in [a]
manner, by violence enforced to let books to be
made, not by you, but by profane and lay persons ;
to let them, I say, be sold abroad, and read for
the instruction of the people ? I am bold with you,
but I speak Latin and not English, to the clergy,
not to the laity ; I speak to you being present,
and not behind your backs. God is my witness,
I speak whatsoever is spoken of the goodwill that
I bear you ; God is my witness, which knoweth
my heart, and compelleth me to say that I say.

Now, I pray you in God's name, what did you,
so great fathers, so many, so long a season, so oft
assembled together ? What went you about ?
What would ye have brought to pass ? Two
things taken away—the one, that ye (which I
heard) burned a dead man ; [2] the other, that ye

[1] See the king's letter to his bishops directing them how to
instruct the people. Wilkins, *Concil.* iii. 825 (*Corrie*).

[2] The will of William Tracy, of Toddington, Worcester, did not
ecommend his soul to the intercession of the saints. Tracy was
therefore pronounced by Convocation to be a heretic, and his body
was taken up and burned. This was in 1532.

(which I felt) went about to burn one being alive : [1]
him, because he did, I cannot tell how, in his
testament withstand your profit ; in other points,
as I have heard, a very good man ; reported to be
of an honest life while he lived, full of good works,
good both to the clergy, and also to the laity :
this order, which truly never hurt any of you, ye
would have raked in the coals, because he would
not subscribe to certain articles that took away
the supremacy of the king :——take away these two
noble acts, and there is nothing else left that ye
went about, that I know, saving that I now
remember, that somewhat ye attempted against
Erasmus,[2] albeit as yet nothing is come to light.
Ye have oft sat in consultation, but what have ye
done ? Ye have had many things in deliberation,
but what one is put forth, whereby either Christ
is more glorified, or else Christ's people made
more holy?

I appeal to your own conscience. How
chanced this ? How came it thus ? Because
there were no children of light, no children of
God amongst you, which, setting the world at
nought, would study to illustrate the glory of God,
and thereby shew themselves children of light ?
I think not so, certainly I think not so. God
forbid, that all you, which were gathered

---

[1] Latimer himself was summoned before Convocation in 1532.

[2] Standish, afterwards Bishop of St Asaph, charged Erasmus
with heresy in 1520 ; but nothing came of it.

together under the pretence of light, should
children of the world ! Then why happened thi
Why, I pray you ? Perchance, either because t
children of the world were more in number
this your congregation, as it oft happeneth, or
the least of more policy than the children
light in their generation : whereby it might ver
soon be brought to pass, that these were much
more stronger in gendering the evil, than these in
producing the good. The children of light have
policy, but it is like the policy of the serpent, and
is joined with doveish simplicity. They engender
nothing but simply, faithfully, and plainly, even
so doing all that they do. And therefore they
may with more facility be cumbered in their
engendering, and be the more ready to take injuries.
But the children of this world have worldly policy,
foxly craft, lion-like cruelty, power to do hurt,
more than either *aspis* or *basiliscus*, engendering
and doing all things fraudulently, deceitfully,
guilefully : which as Nimrods and such sturdy
and stout hunters, being full of simulation and
dissimulation before the Lord, deceive the children
of light, and cumber them easily. Hunters go
not forth in every man's sight, but do their affairs
closely, and with use of guile and deceit wax
every day more craftier than other.

The children of this world be like crafty hunters ;
they be misnamed children of light, forasmuch as
they so hate light, and so study to do the works

of darkness. If they were the children of light,
they would not love darkness. It is no marvel
that they go about to keep other in darkness,
seeing they be in darkness, from top to toe over-
whelmed with darkness, darker than is the darkness of hell. Wherefore it is well done in all
orders of men, but especial in the order of prelates,
to put a difference between children of light and
children of the world, because great deceit ariseth
in taking the one for the other. Great imposture
cometh, when they that the common people take
for the light, go about to take the sun and the
light out of the world. But these be easily known,
both by the diversity of minds, and also their
armours. For whereas the children of light are
thus minded, that they seek their adversaries'
health, wealth, and profit, with loss of their own
commodities, and ofttimes with jeopardy of their
life ; the children of the world, contrariwise, have
such stomachs, that they will sooner see them
dead that doth them good, than sustain any loss
of temporal things.

The armour of the children of light are, first,
the word of God, which they ever set forth, and
with all diligence put it abroad, that, as much as
in them lieth, it may bring forth fruit : after this,
patience and prayer, with the which in all
adversities the Lord comforteth them. Other
things they commit to God, unto whom they leave
all revengement. The armour of the children of

the world are, sometimes frauds and deceits, sometimes lies and money : by the first they make
their dreams, their traditions ; by the second they
stablish and confirm their dreams, be they never
so absurd, never so against Scripture, honesty, or
reason. And if any man resist them, even with
these weapons they procure to slay him. Thus
they bought Christ's death, the very light itself,
and obscured Him after His death : thus they
buy every day the children of light, and
obscure them, and shall so do, until the world
be at an end. So that it may be ever true,
that Christ said : ' The children of the world
be wiser,' &c.

These worldlings pull down the lively faith, and
full confidence that men have in Christ, and set
up another faith, another confidence, of their own
making : the children of light contrary. These
worldlings set little by such works as God hath
prepared for our salvation, but they extol traditions
and works of their own invention : the children of
light contrary. The worldlings, if they spy profit,
gains, or lucre in any thing, be it never such a
trifle, be it never so pernicious, they preach it to
the people, (if they preach at any time,) and these
things they defend with tooth and nail. They
can scarce disallow the abuses of these, albeit
they be intolerable, lest in disallowing the abuse
they lose part of their profit. The children of the
light contrary, put all things in their degree, best

highest, next next, the worst lowest. They extol things necessary, Christian, and commanded of God. They pull down will-works feigned by men, and put them in their place. The abuses of all things they earnestly rebuke. But yet these things be so done on both parties, and so they both do gender, that the children of the world shew themselves wiser than the children of light, and that frauds and deceits, lies and money, seem evermore to have the upper hand. I hold my peace; I will not say how fat feasts and jolly banquets be jolly instruments to set forth worldly matters withal. Neither the children of the world be only wiser than the children of light, but are also some of them among themselves much wiser than the other in their generation. For albeit, as touching the end, the generation of them all is one; yet in this same generation some of them have more craftily engendered than the other of their fellows.

For what a thing was that, that once every hundred year was brought forth in Rome of the children of this world, and with how much policy it was made, ye heard at Paul's Cross[1] in the beginning of the last parliament: how some brought forth canonizations, some expectations,[2]

[1] The Preaching-place so powerful during the Reformation. A stone in St Paul's Churchyard now marks the site.

[2] *Gratiæ expectivæ*, or certain papal instruments by which benefices, not yet vacant, were prospectively made over to purchasers. Many laws were enacted in England against this intolerable abuse (*Corrie*).

some pluralities and unions,[1] some tot-quots [2] and dispensations, some pardons, and these of wonderful variety, some stationaries,[3] some jubilaries,[4] some poculuries for drinkers, some manuaries for handlers of relicks, some pedaries for pilgrims, some osculuries for kissers [5]; some of them engendered one, some other such fetures,[6] and every one in that he was delivered of, was excellent politic, wise ; yea, so wise, that with their wisdom they had almost made all the world fools.

But yet they that begot and brought forth that our old ancient purgatory pick-purse ; that that was swaged [7] and cooled with a Franciscan's cowl, put upon a dead man's back, to the fourth part of his sins [8]; that that was utterly to be spoiled, and of none other but of our most prudent lord Pope, and of him as oft as him listed ; that satisfactory, that missal, that scalary,[9] they, I say, that were the wise fathers and genitors of this purgatory, were in my mind the wisest of

[1] i.e. of benefices.

[2] Tot-quots, toties-quoties, a general dispensation.

[3] Litanies and masses sung on certain fixed days for the remission of sins.

[4] Jubilees were a source of revenue to the Papal See.

[5] Consecrated drinking-vessels, gloves, sandals and tablets bearing representations of our Lord or of a saint—all articles of ecclesiastical commerce.

[6] Fetures : offspring or production, fetura.

[7] Swaged, i.e. assuaged.

[8] To be buried in the garb of St Francis was to earn so much pardon.

[9] Scalary, masses of scala cœli.

all their generation, and so far pass the children of light, and also the rest of their company, that they both are but fools, if ye compare them with these. It was a pleasant fiction, and from the beginning so profitable to the feigners of it, that almost, I dare boldly say, there hath been no emperor that hath gotten more by taxes and tallages of them that were alive, than these, the very and right-begotten sons of the world, got by dead men's tributes and gifts. If there be some in England, that would this sweeting of the world to be with no less policy kept still than it was born and brought forth in Rome, who then can accuse Christ of lying?

No, no; as it hath been ever true, so it shall be, that the children of the world be much wiser, not only in making their things, but also in conserving them. I wot not what it is, but somewhat it is I wot, that some men be so loth to see the abuse of this monster, purgatory, which abuse is more than abominable: as who should say, there is none abuse in it, or else as though there can be none in it. They may seem heartily to love the old thing, that thus earnestly endeavour them to restore him his old name. They would not set an hair by the name, but for the thing. They be not so ignorant, (no, they be crafty,) but that they know if the name come again, the thing will come after. Thereby it ariseth, that some men make their cracks, that

they, maugre all men's heads, have found
purgatory. I cannot tell what is found. This,
to pray for dead folks, this is not found, for it
was never lost. How can that be found that was
not lost? O subtle finders, that can find things,
if God will, ere they be lost! For that cowlish
deliverance, their scalary loosings, their papal
spoliations, and other such their figments, they
cannot find. No, these be so lost, as they
themselves grant, that though they seek them
never so diligently, yet they shall not find them,
except perchance they hope to see them come in
again with their names; and that then money-
gathering may return again, and deceit walk
about the country, and so stablish their kingdom
in all kingdoms. But to what end this chiding
between the children of the world and the
children of light will come, only He knoweth
that once shall judge them both.

Now, to make haste and to come somewhat
nigher the end. Go ye to, good brethren and
fathers, for the love of God, go ye to; and seeing
we are here assembled, let us do something
whereby we may be known to be the children of
light. Let us do somewhat, lest we, which
hitherto have been judged children of the world,
seem even still to be so. All men call us
prelates: then, seeing we be in council, let us so
order ourselves, that we be prelates in honour and
dignity; so we may be prelates in holiness,

benevolence, diligence, and sincerity. All men know that we be here gathered, and with most fervent desire they anheale,[1] breathe, and gape for the fruit of our convocation : as our acts shall be, so they shall name us : so that now it lieth in us, whether we will be called children of the world, or children of light.

Wherefore lift up your heads, brethren, and look about with your eyes, spy what things are to be reformed in the Church of England. Is it so hard, is it so great a matter for you to see many abuses in the clergy, many in the laity? What is done in the Arches?[2] Nothing to be amended? What do they there? Do they evermore rid the people's business and matters, or cumber and ruffle them? Do they evermore correct vice, or else defend it, sometime being well corrected in other places? How many sentences be given there in time, as they ought to be? If men say truth, how many without bribes? Or if all things be well done there, what do men in bishops' Consistories?[3] Shall you often see the punishments assigned by the laws executed, or else money-redemptions used in their stead? How think you by the ceremonies

[1] Anheale, pant for.

[2] The chief and most ancient Consistory court belonging to the archbishop of Canterbury. The name is derived from the Court having been formerly held in the church of St Mary *le bow*, (*S. Maria de Arcubus*). Blackstone, Comm. xv. 3, c. v. (*Corrie*).

[3] The Court of a Bishop for the trial of ecclesiastical causes.

that are in England, oft-times, with no little
offence of weak consciences, contemned ; more
oftener with superstition so defiled, and so
depraved, that you may doubt whether it were
better some of them to tarry still, or utterly to
take them away ?   Have not our forefathers
complained of the ceremonies, of the superstition,
and estimation of them ?

Do ye see nothing in our holidays ? of the
which very few were made at the first, and they
to set forth goodness, virtue, and honesty : but
sithens, in some places, there is neither mean nor
measure in making new holidays, as who should
say, this one thing is serving of God, to make
this law, that no man may work.   But what doth
the people on these holidays ?   Do they give
themselves to godliness, or else ungodliness ?
See ye nothing, brethren ?   If you see not, yet
God seeth.   God seeth all the whole holidays to
be spent miserably in drunkenness, in glossing,
in strife, in envy, in dancing, dicing, idleness, and
gluttony.

He seeth all this, and threateneth punishment
for it.   He seeth it, which neither is deceived in
seeing nor deceiveth when He threateneth.

Thus men serve the devil ; for God is not thus
served, albeit ye say ye serve God.   No, the devil
hath more service done unto him on one holiday,
than on many working days.   Let all these abuses
be counted as nothing, who is he that is not sorry

to see in so many holidays rich and wealthy persons to flow in delicates, and men that live by their travail, poor men, to lack necessary meat and drink for their wives and their children, and that they cannot labour upon the holidays, except they will be cited, and brought before our Officials? Were it not the office of good prelates to consult upon these matters, and to seek some remedy for them? Ye shall see, my brethren, ye shall see once, what will come of this our winking.

What think ye of these images that are had more than their fellows in reputation; that are gone unto with such labour and weariness of the body, frequented with such our cost, sought out and visited with such confidence? What say ye by these images, that are so famous, so noble, so noted, being of them so many and so divers in England? Do you think that this preferring of picture to picture, image to image, is the right use, and not rather the abuse, of images? But you will say to me, Why make ye all these interrogations? and why, in these your demands, do you let and withdraw the good devotion of the people? Be not all things well done, that are done with good intent, when they be profitable to us? So, surely, covetousness both thinketh and speaketh. Were it not better for us, more for estimation, more meeter for men in our places, to cut away a piece of this our profit, if we will not cut away all, than to wink at such ungodliness, and so long to

wink for a little lucre ; specially if it be ungodliness, and also seem unto you ungodliness ? These
be two things, so oft to seek mere images, and
sometime to visit the relics of saints. And yet,
as in those there may be much ungodliness committed, so there may here some superstition be
hid, if that sometime we chance to visit pigs'
bones instead of saints' relics, as in time past it
hath chanced, I had almost said, in England.

Then this is too great a blindness, a darkness
too sensible, that these should be so commended
in sermons of some men, and preached to be done
after such manner, as though they could not be
evil done ; which, notwithstanding, are such, that
neither God nor man commandeth them to be
done. No, rather, men commanded them either
not to be done at all, or else more slowlier and
seldomer to be done, forasmuch as our ancestors
made this constitution : ' We command the priests,
that they oft admonish the people, and in especial
women, that they make no vows but after long
deliberation, consent of their husbands, and counsel
of the priest.' [1]   The Church of England in time

---

[1] The constitution alluded to is attributed to Edmund, archbishop
of Canterbury in the year 1236. *Præcipimus ut sacerdotes sæpe
moneant populum, et maxime mulieres, ne faciant vota sua nisi
cum deliberatione et de consensu virorum suorum et concilio sacer-
dotum. Lyndewode, Provincial*, p. 204, Oxon. 1679. See also
Wilkins, *Concil.* i. p. 638. But the constitution is actually of much
older date, being found, in substance, in the *Pænitentiale of
Theodore*, cap. xvi. v. 23. *Ancient Laws and Institutes of
England*, vol. ii. p. 11, 8vo. Edit. 1840. (*Corrie.*)

past made this constitution. What saw they that made this decree? They saw the intolerable abuses of images. They saw the perils that might ensue of going on pilgrimage. They saw the superstitious difference that men made between image and image. Surely, somewhat they saw. The constitution is so made, that in manner it taketh away all such pilgrimages. For it so plucketh away the abuse of them, that it leaveth either none, or else seldom use of them. For they that restrain making vows for going of pilgrimage, restrain also pilgrimage ; seeing that for the most part it is seen that few go on pilgrimage but vow-makers, and such as by promise bind themselves to go.

And when, I pray you, should a man's wife go on pilgrimage, if she went not before she had well debated the matter with herself, and obtained the consent of her husband, being a wise man, and were also counselled by a learned priest so to do? When should she go far off to these famous images? For this the common people of England think to be going on pilgrimage ; to go to some dead and notable image out of town, that is to say, far from their house. Now, if your forefathers made this constitution, and yet thereby did nothing, the abuses every day more and more increased, what is left for you to do? Brethren and fathers, if ye purpose to do any thing, what should ye sooner do, than to take

F

utterly away these deceitful and juggling images;
or else, if ye know any other mean to put away
abuses, to shew it, if ye intend to remove abuses?
Methink it should be grateful and pleasant to you
to mark the earnest mind of your forefathers, and
to look upon their desire where they say in their
constitution, 'We *command* you,' and not, 'We
counsel you.' How have we been so long a-cold,
so long slack in setting forth so wholesome a
precept of the church of England, where we be
so hot in all things that have any gains in them,
albeit they be neither commanded us, nor yet
given us by counsel; as though we had lever the
abuse of things should tarry still than, it taken
away, lose our profit? To let pass the solemn
and nocturnal bacchanals, the prescript miracles,
that are done upon certain days in the west part
of England, who hath not heard? I think ye
have heard of St Blesis's heart which is at
Malverne, and of St Algar's bones, how long
they deluded the people: I am afraid, to the loss
of many souls. Whereby men may well con-
jecture, that all about in this realm there is
plenty of such juggling deceits. And yet hitherto
ye have sought no remedy. But even still the
miserable people are suffered to take the false
miracles for the true, and to lie still asleep in
all kind of superstition. God have mercy upon us!
    Last of all, how think you of matrimony? Is
all well here? What of baptism? Shall we

ever more in ministering of it speak Latin, and
not in English rather, that the people may know
what is said and done?

What think ye of these mass-priests, and of
the masses themselves? What say ye? Be all
things here so without abuses, that nothing ought
to be amended? Your forefathers saw somewhat,
which made this constitution against the venality
and sale of masses, that, under pain of suspending,
no priest should sell his saying of tricennals[1] or
annals.[2] What saw they, that made this constitution? What priests saw they? What manner
of masses saw they, trow ye? But at the last,
what became of so good a constitution? God
have mercy upon us! If there be nothing to be
amended abroad, concerning the whole, let every
one of us make one better: if there be neither
abroad nor at home any thing to be amended
and redressed, my lords, be ye of good cheer, be
merry; and at the least, because we have nothing
else to do, let us reason the matter how we may
be richer.

Let us fall to some pleasant communication;
after let us go home, even as good as we came
hither, that is, right-begotten children of the
world, and utterly worldlings. And while we

[1] Tricennals or *Trentals*—Thirty masses said daily for a dead
person during one month after his decease. Johnson, *Eccles.
Laws*, II.

[2] *Annals*, or *Annuals*, a yearly mass said for a certain dead
person, upon the anniversary of his death.

live here, let us all make bone cheer. For after this life there is small pleasure, little mirth for us to hope for ; if now there be nothing to be changed in our fashions. Let us say, not as St Peter did, 'Our end approacheth nigh,' this is an heavy hearing ; but let us say as the evil servant said, 'It will be long ere my master come.' This is pleasant. Let us beat our fellows : let us eat and drink with drunkards. Surely, as oft as we do not take away the abuse of things, so oft we beat our fellows. As oft as we give not the people their true food, so oft we beat our fellows. As oft as we let them die in superstition, so oft we beat them. To be short, as oft as we blind lead them blind, so oft we beat, and grievously beat our fellows. When we welter in pleasures and idleness, then we eat and drink with drunkards. But God will come, God will come, He will not tarry long away. He will come upon such a day as we nothing look for Him, and at such hour as we know not. He will come and cut us in pieces. He will reward us as He doth the hypocrites. He will set us where wailing shall be, my brethren ; where gnashing of teeth shall be, my brethren. And let here be the end of our tragedy, if ye will.

These be the delicate dishes prepared for the world's well-beloved children. These be the wafers and junkets provided for worldly prelates, —wailing and gnashing of teeth. Can there be any mirth, where these two courses last all the feast? Here we laugh, there we shall weep. Our teeth make merry here, ever dashing in delicates; there shall be torn with teeth, and do nothing but gnash and grind our own. To what end have we now excelled other in policy? What have we brought forth at the last? Ye see, brethren, what sorrow, what punishment is provided for you, if ye be worldlings. If ye will not thus be vexed, be ye not the children of the world. If ye will not be the children of the world, be not stricken with the love of worldly things; lean not upon them. If ye will not die eternally, live not worldly. Come, go to; leave the love of your profit; study for the glory and profit of Christ; seek in your consultations such things as pertain to Christ, and bring forth at the last somewhat that may please Christ. Feed ye tenderly, with all diligence, the flock of Christ. Preach truly the word of God. Love the light, walk in the light, and so be ye the children of light while ye are in this world, that ye may shine in the world that is to come bright as the sun, with the Father, the Son, and the Holy Ghost; to whom be all honour, praise, and glory. Amen.

THE SERMON OF THE PLOUGH.[1]

Romans xv. 4.—'Whatsoever things were written aforetime were written for our learning.'

'ALL things which are written, are written for our erudition and knowledge. All things that are written in God's book, in the Bible book, in the book of the holy scripture, are written to be our doctrine.'

I told you in my first sermon, honourable audience, that I purposed to declare unto you two things. The one, what seed should be sown in God's field, in God's plough land; and the other, who should be the sowers: that is to say, what doctrine is to be taught in Christ's church and congregation, and what men should be the teachers and preachers of it. The first part I have told you in the three sermons past, in which I have assayed to set forth my plough, to prove what I could do. And now I shall tell you who be the ploughers: for God's word is a seed to be

[1] Preached 'in the Shrouds at Paul's Church'—*i.e.* in a covered place by the side of the Cathedral used when the weather was too inclement for hearers at Paul's Cross—on January 18, 1548. Apparently this was the last of a series of four. It is perhaps the best known of all Latimer's sermons.

sown in God's field, that is, the faithful congregation, and the preacher is the sower. And it is in the gospel : *Exivit qui seminat seminare semen suum ;* 'He that soweth, the husbandman, the ploughman, went forth to sow his seed.'[1] So that a preacher is resembled to a ploughman, as it is in another place : *Nemo admota aratro manu, et a tergo respiciens, aptus est regno Dei.* 'No man that putteth his hand to the plough, and looketh back, is apt for the kingdom of God.'[2] That is to say, let no preacher be negligent in doing his office. Albeit this is one of the places that hath been racked,[3] as I told you of racking scriptures. And I have been one of them myself that hath racked it, I cry God mercy for it ; and have been one of them that have believed and expounded it against religious persons that would forsake their order which they had professed, and would go out of their cloister : whereas indeed it toucheth not monkery, nor maketh any thing at all for any such matter ; but it is directly spoken of diligent preaching of the word of God.

For preaching of the gospel is one of God's plough-works, and the preacher is one of God's ploughmen. Ye may not be offended with my similitude, in that I compare preaching to the labour and work of ploughing, and the preacher

---

[1] Luke viii. 5. [2] Luke ix. 62.
[3] Wrested, strained like one upon the rack.

to a ploughman : ye may not be offended with this my similitude ; for I have been slandered of some persons for such things. It hath been said of me, 'Oh, Latimer ! nay, as for him, I will never believe him while I live, nor never trust him ; for he likened our blessed lady to a saffron-bag :' where indeed I never used that similitude. But it was, as I have said unto you before now, according to that which Peter saw before in the spirit of prophecy, and said, that there should come after men *per quos via veritatis maledictis afficeretur ;* there should come fellows 'by whom the way of truth should be evil spoken of, and slandered."[1] But in case I had used this similitude, it had not been to be reproved, but might have been without reproach. For I might have said thus : as the saffron-bag that hath been full of saffron, or hath had saffron in it, doth ever after savour and smell of the sweet saffron that it contained ; so our blessed lady, which conceived and bare Christ in her womb, did ever after resemble the manners and virtues of that precious babe that she bare. And what had our blessed lady been the worse for this ? Or what dishonour was this to our blessed lady ?

But as preachers must be wary and circumspect, that they give not any just occasion to be slandered and ill spoken of by the hearers, so must not the auditors be offended without cause. For

[1] 2 Peter ii. 2.

heaven is in the gospel likened to a mustard-seed :
it is compared also to a piece of leaven ; and as
Christ saith, that at the last day He will come
like a thief : and what dishonour is this to God ?
or what derogation is this to heaven ? Ye may
not then, I say, be offended with my similitude,
for because I liken preaching to a ploughman's
labour, and a prelate to a ploughman.

But now you will ask me, whom I call a
prelate ? A prelate is that man, whatsoever he
be, that hath a flock to be taught of him ; whosoever hath any spiritual charge in the faithful
congregation, and whosoever he be that hath cure
of souls. And well may the preacher and the
ploughman be likened together : first, for their
labour of all seasons of the year ; for there is no
time of the year in which the ploughman hath
not some special work to do : as in my country
in Leicestershire, the ploughman hath a time to
set forth, and to assay his plough, and other times
for other necessary works to be done. And then
they also may be likened together for the diversity of works and variety of offices that they have
to do. For as the ploughman first setteth forth
his plough, and then tilleth his land, and breaketh
it in furrows, and sometime ridgeth it up again ;
and at another time harroweth it and clotteth it,
and sometime dungeth it and hedgeth it, diggeth
it and weedeth it, purgeth and maketh it clean :
so the prelate, the preacher, hath many diverse

offices to do. He hath first a busy work to bring his parishioners to a right faith, as Paul calleth it, and not a swerving faith ; but to a faith that embraceth Christ, and trusteth to His merits ; a lively faith, a justifying faith ; a faith that maketh a man righteous, without respect of works : as ye have it very well declared and set forth in the Homily.[1]

He hath then a busy work, I say, to bring his flock to a right faith, and then to confirm them in the same faith : now casting them down with the law, and with threatenings of God for sin ; now ridging them up again with the gospel, and with the promises of God's favour : now weeding them, by telling them their faults, and making them forsake sin ; now clotting them, by breaking their stony hearts, and by making them supple-hearted, and making them to have hearts of flesh ; that is, soft hearts, and apt for doctrine to enter in : now teaching to know God rightly, and to know their duty to God and their neighbours : now exhorting them, when they know their duty, that they do it, and be diligent in it ; so that they have a continual work to do. Great is their business, and therefore great should be their hire. They have great labours, and therefore they ought to have good livings, that they may commodiously feed their flock ; for the preaching of the word of God unto the people is called meat :

[1] 'A Short Declaration of the True, Lively, and Christian Faith.'

scripture calleth it meat; not strawberries,[1] that
come but once a year, and tarry not long, but
are soon gone: but it is meat, it is no dainties.
The people must have meat that must be familiar
and continual, and daily given unto them to feed
upon. Many make a strawberry of it, ministering
it but once a year; but such do not the office of
good prelates. For Christ saith, *Quis putas est
servus prudens et fidelis? Qui dat cibum in tempore.*
'Who think you is a wise and faithful servant?
He that giveth meat in due time.'[2] So that he
must at all times convenient preach diligently:
therefore saith he, 'Who trow ye is a faithful
servant?' He speaketh it as though it were a
rare thing to find such a one, and as though he
should say, there be but a few of them to find in
the world. And how few of them there be
throughout this realm that give meat to their
flock as they should do, the Visitors can best tell.
Too few, too few; the more is the pity, and
never so few as now.

By this, then, it appeareth that a prelate, or

---

[1] This expression which Latimer made use of to designate the non-
residents of his day, who only visited their cures once a year,
became proverbial. A bachelor of divinity, named Oxenbridge, in
a sermon preached at St Paul's Cross, Jan. 13, 1566, says, ' I will
shew you the state and condition of this my mother Oxford; for a
pitious case it is, that now in all Oxford there is not past five or
six preachers, I except strawberry preachers.' WATKINS:
Latimer's Sermons, i. 58, note.

[2] Matt. xxiv. 45.

any that hath cure of soul, must diligently and substantially work and labour. Therefore saith Paul to Timothy, *Qui episcopatum desiderat, hic bonum opus desiderat:* ' He that desireth to have the office of a bishop, or a prelate, that man desireth a good work.'[1] Then if it be a good work, it is work ; ye can make but a work of it. It is God's work, God's plough, and that plough God would have still going. Such then as loiter and live idly, are not good prelates, or ministers. And of such as do not preach and teach, nor do their duties, God saith by his prophet Jeremy, *Maledictus qui facit opus Dei fradulenter;* 'Cursed be the man that doth the work of God fraudulently, guilefully or deceitfully :'[2] some books have it *negligenter,* ' negligently or slackly.' How many such prelates, how many such bishops, Lord, for Thy mercy, are there now in England ! And what shall we in this case do ? shall we company with them ? O Lord, for Thy mercy ! shall we not company with them ? O Lord, whither shall we flee from them ? But ' cursed be he that doth the work of God negligently or guilefully.' A sore word for them that are negligent in discharging their office, or have done it fraudulently ; for that is the thing that maketh the people ill.

But true it must be that Christ saith, *Multi sunt vocati, pauci vero electi :* ' Many are called,

[1] 1 Tim. iii. 1.   [2] Jer. xlviii. 10.

but few are chosen.'[1] Here have I an occasion by
the way somewhat to say unto you ; yea, for the
place I alleged unto you before out of Jeremy,
the forty-eighth chapter. And it was spoken of
a spiritual work of God, a work that was commanded to be done ; and it was of shedding
blood, and of destroying the cities of Moab. For,
saith he, 'Cursed be he that keepeth back his
sword from shedding of blood.' As Saul, when
he kept back the sword from shedding of blood
at what time he was sent against Amaleck, was
refused of God for being disobedient to God's
commandment, in that he spared Agag the king.
So that that place of the prophet was spoken of
them that went to the destruction of the cities of
Moab, among the which there was one called
Nebo, which was much reproved for idolatry,
superstition, pride, avarice, cruelty, tyranny, and
for hardness of heart ; and for these sins was
plagued by God and destroyed.

Now what shall we say of these rich citizens
of London ? What shall I say of them ? Shall
I call them proud men of London, malicious
men of London, merciless men of London ? No,
no, I may not say so ; they will be offended with
me then. Yet must I speak. For is there not
reigning in London as much pride, as much
covetousness, as much cruelty, as much oppression, and as much superstition, as was in Nebo ?

[1] Matt. xxii. 14.

Yes, I think, and much more too.   Therefore
I say, repent, O London ; repent, repent.   Thou
hearest thy faults told thee, amend them, amend
them.   I think, if Nebo had had the preaching
that thou hast, they would have converted.   And,
you rulers and officers, be wise and circumspect,
look to your charge, and see you do your duties ;
and rather be glad to amend your ill living than to
be angry when you are warned or told of your fault.

What ado was there made in London at a
certain man, because he said (and indeed at that
on a just cause), 'Burgesses !' quoth he, 'nay,
Butterflies.'   Lord, what ado there was for that
word !   And yet, would God they were no worse
than butterflies !   Butterflies do but their nature :
the butterfly is not covetous, is not greedy, of
other men's goods ; is not full of envy and
hatred, is not malicious, is not cruel, is not
merciless.   The butterfly glorieth not in her
own deeds, nor preferreth the traditions of men
before God's word ; it committeth not idolatry,
nor worshippeth false gods.

But London cannot abide to be rebuked ; such
is the nature of man.   If they be pricked, they
will kick ; if they be rubbed on the gall, they will
wince ; but yet they will not amend their faults,
they will not be ill spoken of.   But how shall I
speak well of them ?   If you could be content to
receive and follow the word of God, and favour
good preachers, if you could bear to be told of

your faults, if you could amend when you hear of
them, if you would be glad to reform that is
amiss ; if I might see any such inclination in you,
that you would leave to be merciless, and begin
to be charitable, I would then hope well of you,
I would then speak well of you.

But London was never so ill as it is now.   In
times past men were full of pity and compassion,
but now there is no pity ; for in London their
brother shall die in the streets for cold, he shall
lie sick at the door between stock and stock, I
cannot tell what to call it, and perish there for
hunger : was there ever more unmercifulness in
Nebo?   I think not.   In times past, when any
rich man died in London, they were wont to
help the poor scholars of the Universities with
exhibition.   When any man died, they would
bequeath great sums of money toward the relief
of the poor.   When I was a scholar in Cambridge
myself, I heard very good report of London, and
knew many that had relief of the rich men of
London : but now I can hear no such good
report, and yet I inquire of it, and hearken for it;
but now charity is waxen cold, none helpeth the
scholar, nor yet the poor.   And in those days,
what did they when they helped the scholars?
Marry, they maintained and gave them livings
that were very papists, and professed the pope's
doctrine : and now that the knowledge of God's
word is brought to light, and many earnestly

study and labour to set it forth, now almost no man helpeth to maintain them.

Oh London, London! repent, repent; for I think God is more displeased with London than ever he was with the city of Nebo. Repent therefore, repent, London, and remember that the same God liveth now that punished Nebo, even the same God, and none other; and He will punish sin as well now as He did then : and He will punish the iniquity of London, as well as He did then of Nebo. Amend therefore. And ye that be prelates, look well to your office; for right prelating is busy labouring, and not lording. Therefore preach and teach, and let your plough be doing. Ye lords, I say, that live like loiterers, look well to your office ; the plough is your office and charge. If you live idle and loiter, you do not your duty, you follow not your vocation : let your plough therefore be going, and not cease, that the ground may bring forth fruit.

But now methinketh I hear one say unto me : Wot ye what you say? Is it a work? Is it a labour? How then hath it happened that we have had so many hundred years so many un-preaching prelates, lording loiterers, and idle ministers? Ye would have me here to make answer, and to shew the cause thereof. Nay, this land is not for me to plough; it is too stony, too thorny, too hard for me to plough. They have so many things that make for them, so many things to lay for themselves, that it is not for my weak team to plough them. They have to lay for themselves long customs, ceremonies and authority, placing in parliament, and many things more. And I fear me this land is not yet ripe to be ploughed: for, as the saying is, it lacketh weathering: this gear lacketh weathering; at least way it is not for me to plough. For what shall I look for among thorns, but pricking and scratching? What among stones, but stumbling? What (I had almost said) among serpents, but stinging?

But this much I dare say, that since lording and loitering hath come up, preaching hath come down, contrary to the apostles' times: for they preached and lorded not, and now they lord and preach not. For they that be lords will ill go to plough: it is no meet office for them; it is not seeming for their estate. Thus came up lording loiterers: thus crept in unpreaching prelates; and so have they long continued. For how many unlearned prelates have we now at this day! And no marvel: for if the ploughmen that now be were made lords, they would clean give over ploughing; they would leave off their labour, and fall to lording outright, and let the plough stand: and then both ploughs not walking, nothing should be in the commonweal but hunger. For ever since the prelates were made lords and nobles, the plough standeth; there is no work done, the people starve. They hawk, they hunt,

G

they card, they dice ; they pastime in their prelacies with gallant gentlemen, with their dancing minions, and with their fresh companions, so that ploughing is set aside : and by their lording and loitering, preaching and ploughing is clean gone. And thus if the ploughmen of the country were as negligent in their office as prelates be, we should not long live, for lack of sustenance. And as it is necessary for to have this ploughing for the sustentation of the body, so must we have also the other for the satisfaction of the soul, or else we cannot live long ghostly. For as the body wasteth and consumeth away for lack of bodily meat, so doth the soul pine away for default of ghostly meat. But there be two kinds of inclosing, to let or hinder both these kinds of ploughing ; the one is an inclosing to let or hinder the bodily ploughing, and the other to let or hinder the holiday-ploughing, the church-ploughing.

The bodily ploughing is taken in and inclosed through singular commodity. For what man will let go, or diminish his private commodity for a commonwealth ? And who will sustain any damage for the respect of a public commodity ? The other plough also no man is diligent to set forward, nor no man will hearken to it. But to hinder and let it all men's ears are open ; yea, and a great many of this kind of ploughmen, which are very busy, and would seem to be very good workmen. I fear me some be rather mock-gospellers, than faithful ploughmen. I know many myself that profess the gospel, and live nothing thereafter. I know them, and have been conversant with some of them. I know them, and (I speak it with a heavy heart) there is as little charity and good living in them as in any other ; according to that which Christ said in the gospel to the great number of people that followed him, as though they had had any earnest zeal to his doctrine, whereas indeed they had it not ; *Non quia vidistis signa, sed quia comedistis de panibus.*[1] 'Ye follow Me,' saith He, 'not because ye have seen the signs and miracles that I have done ; but because ye have eaten the bread, and refreshed your bodies, therefore you follow me.' So that I think many one now-a-days professeth the gospel for the living's sake, not for the love they bear to God's word. But they that will be true ploughmen must work faithfully for God's sake, for the edifying of their brethren. And as diligently as the husbandman plougheth for the sustentation of the body, so diligently must the prelates and ministers labour for the feeding of the soul : both the ploughs must still be going, as most necessary for man. And wherefore are magistrates ordained, but that the tranquillity of the commonweal may be confirmed, limiting both ploughs ?

But now for the fault of unpreaching prelates,

[1] John vi. 26.

methink I could guess what might be said for excusing of them. They are so troubled with lordly living, they be so placed in palaces, couched in courts, ruffling in their rents, dancing in their dominions, burdened with ambassages, pampering of their paunches, like a monk that maketh his jubilee ; munching in their mangers, and moiling [1] in their gay manors and mansions, and so troubled with loitering in their lordships, that they cannot attend it.   They are otherwise occupied, some in the king's matters, some are ambassadors, some of the privy council, some to furnish the court, some are lords of the parliament, some are presidents, and comptrollers of mints.

Well, well, is this their duty ?   Is this their office ?   Is this their calling ?   Should we have ministers of the church to be comptrollers of the mints ?   Is this a meet office for a priest that hath cure of souls ?   Is this his charge ?   I would here ask one question : I would fain know who controlleth the devil at home in his parish, while he controlleth the mint ?   If the apostles might not leave the office of preaching to the deacons, shall one leave it for minting ?   I cannot tell you ;   but the saying is, that since priests have been minters, money hath been worse than it was before.   And they say that the evilness of money hath made all things dearer.   And in this behalf I must speak to England.   'Hear, my country,

---

[1] Moiling, wallowing.

England,' as Paul said in his first epistle to the
Corinthians, the sixth chapter ; for Paul was no
sitting bishop, but a walking and a preaching
bishop. But when he went from them, he left
there behind him the plough going still ; for he
wrote unto them, and rebuked them for going to
law, and pleading their causes before heathen
judges : ' Is there,' saith he, ' utterly among you
no wise man, to be an arbitrator in matters of
judgment ? What, not one of all that can judge
between brother and brother ; but one brother
goeth to law with another, and that under heathen
judges ? *Constituite contemptos qui sunt in ecclesia*,
etc. Appoint them judges that are most abject
and vile in the congregation.' Which he speaketh
in rebuking them ; ' For,' saith he, *ad erubescentiam
vestram dico*—' I speak it to your shame.' So,
England, I speak it to thy shame : is there never
a nobleman to be a lord president, but it must be
a prelate ? Is there never a wise man in the
realm to be a comptroller of the mint ? ' I speak
it to your shame. I speak it to your shame.' If
there be never a wise man, make a water-bearer,
a tinker, a cobbler, a slave, a page, comptroller of
the mint : make a mean gentleman, a groom, a
yeoman, or a poor beggar, lord president.

Thus I speak, not that I would have it so ; but
' to your shame,' if there be never a gentleman
meet nor able to be lord president. For why
are not the noblemen and young gentlemen of

England so brought up in knowledge of God, and in learning, that they may be able to execute offices in the commonweal? The king hath a great many of wards, and I trow there is a Court of Wards: why is there not a school for the wards, as well as there is a Court for their lands? Why are they not set in schools where they may learn? Or why are they not sent to the universities, that they may be able to serve the king when they come to age? If the wards and young gentlemen were well brought up in learning, and in the knowledge of God, they would not when they come to age so much give themselves to other vanities. And if the nobility be well trained in godly learning, the people would follow the same train. For truly, such as the noblemen be, such will the people be. And now, the only cause why noblemen be not made lord presidents, is because they have not been brought up in learning.

Therefore for the love of God appoint teachers and schoolmasters, you that have charge of youth; and give the teachers stipends worthy their pains, that they may bring them up in grammar, in logic, in rhetoric, in philosophy, in the civil law, and in that which I cannot leave unspoken of, the word of God. Thanks be unto God, the nobility otherwise is very well brought up in learning and godliness, to the great joy and comfort of England; so that there is now good hope in the youth, that we shall another day have a flourishing commonweal, considering their godly education. Yea, and there be already noblemen enough, though not so many as I would wish, able to be lord presidents, and wise men enough for the mint. And as unmeet a thing it is for bishops to be lord presidents, or priests to be minters, as it was for the Corinthians to plead matters of variance before heathen judges. It is also a slander to the noblemen, as though they lacked wisdom and learning to be able for such offices, or else were no men of conscience, or else were not meet to be trusted, and able for such offices. And a prelate hath a charge and cure otherwise ; and therefore he cannot discharge his duty and be a lord president too. For a presidentship requireth a whole man ; and a bishop cannot be two men. A bishop hath his office, a flock to teach, to look unto ; and therefore he cannot meddle with another office, which alone requireth a whole man : he should therefore give it over to whom it is meet, and labour in his own business; as Paul writeth to the Thessalonians, ' Let every man do his own business, and follow his calling.'[1] Let the priest preach, and the nobleman handle the temporal matters. Moses was a marvellous man, a good man : Moses was a wonderful fellow, and did his duty, being a married man : we lack such as Moses was. Well,

[1] Thess. iv. 2.

I would all men would look to their duty, as God hath called them, and then we should have a flourishing Christian commonweal.

And now I would ask a strange question : who is the most diligentest bishop and prelate in all England, that passeth all the rest in doing his office ? I can tell, for I know him who it is ; I know him well. But now I think I see you listening and hearkening that I should name him. There is one that passeth all the other, and is the most diligent prelate and preacher in all England. And will ye know who it is ? I will tell you : it is the devil. He is the most diligent preacher of all other ; he is never out of his diocess ; he is never from his cure ; ye shall never find him unoccupied ; he is ever in his parish ; he keepeth residence at all times ; ye shall never find him out of the way, call for him when you will he is ever at home ; the diligentest preacher in all the realm ; he is ever at his plough : no lording nor loitering can hinder him ; he is ever applying his business, ye shall never find him idle, I warrant you.

And his office is to hinder religion, to maintain superstition, to set up idolatry, to teach all kind of popery. He is ready as he can be wished for to set forth his plough ; to devise as many ways as can be to deface and obscure God's glory. Where the devil is resident, and hath his plough going, there away with books, and up with candles; away with bibles, and up with beads; away with the light of the gospel, and up with the light of candles, yea, at noon-days. Where the devil is resident, that he may prevail, up with all superstition and idolatry; censing, painting of images, candles, palms, ashes, holy water, and new service of men's inventing; as though man could invent a better way to honour God with than God Himself hath appointed. Down with Christ's cross, up with purgatory pickpurse, up with him, the popish purgatory, I mean. Away with clothing the naked, the poor and impotent; up with decking of images, and gay garnishing of stocks and stones: up with man's traditions and his laws, down with God's traditions and His most holy word. Down with the old honour due to God, and up with the new god's honour. Let all things be done in Latin: there must be nothing but Latin, not so much as *Memento, homo, quod cinis es, et in cinerem reverteris :* ' Remember, man, that thou art ashes, and into ashes thou shalt return :' which be the words that the minister speaketh unto the ignorant people, when he giveth them ashes upon Ash-Wednesday; but it must be spoken in Latin: God's word may in no wise be translated into English.

Oh that our prelates would be as diligent to sow the corn of good doctrine, as Satan is to sow cockle and darnel! And this is the devilish ploughing, the which worketh to have things in

Latin, and letteth the fruitful edification. But here some man will say to me, What, sir, are ye so privy of the devil's counsel, that ye know all this to be true? Truly I know him too well, and have obeyed him a little too much in condescending to some follies; and I know him as other men do, yea, that he is ever occupied, and ever busy in following his plough. I know by St Peter, which saith of him, *Sicut leo rugiens circuit quærens quem devoret:* 'He goeth about like a roaring lion, seeking whom he may devour.'[1] I would have this text well viewed and examined, every word of it: '*Circuit*,' he goeth about in every corner of his diocess; he goeth on visitation daily, he leaveth no place of his cure unvisited: he walketh round about from place to place, and ceaseth not. '*Sicut leo*,' as a lion, that is, strongly, boldly, and proudly; stately and fiercely with haughty looks, with his proud countenances, with his stately braggings. '*Rugiens*,' roaring; for he letteth not slip any occasion to speak or to roar out when he seeth his time. *Quærens*, he goeth about seeking, and not sleeping, as our bishops do; but he seeketh diligently, he searcheth diligently all corners, where as he may have his prey. He roveth abroad in every place of his diocess; he standeth not still, he is never at rest, but ever in hand with his plough, that it may go forward.

[1] 1 Pet. v. 8.

But there was never such a preacher in England
as he is. Who is able to tell his diligent preaching, which every day, and every hour, laboureth
to sow cockle and darnel, that he may bring out
of form, and out of estimation and room, the
institution of the Lord's supper and Christ's
cross? For there he lost his right; for Christ
said, *Nunc judicium est mundi, princeps seculi
hujus ejicietur foras. Et sicut exaltavit Moses
serpentem in deserto, ita exaltari oportet Filium
hominis. Et cum exaltatus fuero a terra, omnia
traham ad meipsum.* 'Now is the judgment of
this world, and the prince of this world shall be
cast out. And as Moses did lift up the serpent
in the wilderness, so must the Son of man be lift
up. And when I shall be lift up from the earth,
I will draw all things unto myself.'[1] For the
devil was disappointed of his purpose: for he
thought all to be his own; and when he had
once brought Christ to the cross, he thought all
cocksure. But there lost he all reigning: for
Christ said, *Omnia traham ad meipsum :* 'I will
draw all things to Myself.' He meaneth, drawing
of man's soul to salvation. And that He said
He would do *per semetipsum*, by His own self;
not by any other body's sacrifice. He meant by
His own sacrifice on the cross, where He offered
Himself for the redemption of mankind ; and not
the sacrifice of the mass to be offered by another.

[1] John xii. 31, 32.

For who can offer him but himself? He was both the offerer and the offering.

And this is the prick, this is the mark at the which the devil shooteth, to evacuate the cross of Christ, and to mingle the institution of the Lord's supper; the which although he cannot bring to pass, yet he goeth about by his sleights and subtil means to frustrate the same; and these fifteen hundred years he hath been a doer, only purposing to evacuate Christ's death, and to make it of small efficacy and virtue. For whereas Christ, according as the serpent was lifted up in the wilderness, so would he himself be exalted, that thereby as many as trusted in him should have salvation; but the devil would none of that: they would have us saved by a daily oblation propitiatory, by a sacrifice expiatory, or remissory.

Now if I should preach in the country, among the unlearned, I would tell what propitiatory, expiatory, and remissory is; but here is a learned auditory: yet for them that be unlearned I will expound it. Propitiatory, expiatory, remissory, or satisfactory, for they signify all one thing in effect, and is nothing else but a thing whereby to obtain remission of sins, and to have salvation. And this way the devil used to evacuate the death of Christ, that we might have affiance in other things, as in the sacrifice of the priest; whereas Christ would have us to trust in His only sacrifice. So He was, *Agnus occisus ab origine mundi;* 'The

Lamb that hath been slain from the beginning of the world;'[1] and therefore He is called *juge sacrificium,* 'a continual sacrifice;'[2] and not for the continuance of the mass, as the blanchers have blanched[3] it, and wrested it; and as I myself did once betake it. But Paul saith, *per semetipsum purgatio facta :* 'By Himself,' and by none other, Christ 'made purgation'[4] and satisfaction for the whole world.

Would Christ this word, 'by Himself,' had been better weighed and looked upon, and *in sanctificationem,* to make them holy; for He is *juge sacrificium,* 'a continual sacrifice,' in effect, fruit and operation; that like as they, which seeing the serpent hang up in the desert, were put in remembrance of Christ's death, in whom as many as believed were saved; so all men that trusted in the death of Christ shall be saved, as well they that were before, as they that came after. For He was a continual sacrifice, as I said, in effect, fruit, operation, and virtue; as though He had from the beginning of the world, and continually should to the world's end, hang still on the cross; and He is as fresh hanging on the cross now, to them that believe and trust in Him, as he was fifteen hundred years ago, when He was crucified.

Then let us trust upon His only death, and

---

[1] Rev. xiii. 8.   [2] Dan. viii. 11, 12.
[3] To bleach, or whiten.   [4] Heb. i. 3.

look for none other sacrifice propitiatory, than
the same bloody sacrifice, the lively sacrifice;
and not the dry sacrifice, but a bloody sacrifice.
For Christ Himself said, *consummatum est:* 'It
is perfectly finished! I have taken at my Father's
hand the dispensation of redeeming mankind, I
have wrought man's redemption, and have de-
spatched the matter.' Why then mingle ye
Him? Why do ye divide Him? Why make
you of Him more sacrifices than one? Paul
saith, *Pascha nostrum immolatus est Christus:*
'Christ our passover is offered;'[1] so that the
thing is done, and Christ hath done it, and He
hath done it *semel,* once for all; and it was a
bloody sacrifice, not a dry sacrifice. Why then,
it is not the mass that availeth or profiteth for
the quick and the dead.

Wo worth thee, O devil, wo worth thee, that
hast prevailed so far and so long; that hast made
England to worship false gods, forsaking Christ
their Lord. Wo worth thee, devil, wo worth
thee, devil, and all thy angels. If Christ by His
death draweth all things to Himself, and draweth
all men to salvation, and to heavenly bliss, that
trust in Him; then the priests at the mass, at
the popish mass, I say, what can they draw, when
Christ draweth all, but lands and goods from the
right heirs? The priests draw goods and riches,
benefices and promotions to themselves; and such

[1] Cor. v. 7.

as believed in their sacrifices they draw to the devil. But Christ is He that draweth souls unto Him by His bloody sacrifice. What have we to do then but *epulari in Domino*, to eat in the Lord at His supper? What other service have we to do to Him, and what other sacrifice have we to offer, but the mortification of our flesh? what other oblation have we to make, but of obedience, of good living, of good works, and of helping our neighbours? But as for our redemption, it is done already, it cannot be better : Christ hath done that thing so well, that it cannot be amended. It cannot be devised how to make that any better than He hath done it. But the devil, by the help of that Italian bishop yonder, his chaplain, hath laboured by all means that he might to frustrate the death of Christ and the merits of His passion. And they have devised for that purpose to make us believe in other vain things by His pardons ; as to have remission of sins for praying on hallowed beads ; for drinking of the bakehouse bowl ;[1] as a canon of Waltham Abbey once told me, that whensoever they put their loaves of bread into the oven, as many as drank of the pardon-bowl should have pardon for drinking of it. A mad thing, to give pardon to

---

[1] In the monastery of Bury St Edmund's also was a 'holye relique which was called the *pardon-boule ;* whosoever dronk of this boule in the worshippe of God and Saynt Edmund, he had fiue hundred dayes of pardon, *toties quoties.'* Becon's Works, iii. fol. 187. (*Corrie.*)

a bowl! Then to pope Alexander's[1] holy water, to hallowed bells, palms, candles, ashes, and what not? And of these things, every one hath taken away some part of Christ's sanctification; every one hath robbed some part of Christ's passion and cross, and hath mingled Christ's death, and hath been made to be propitiatory and satisfactory, and to put away sin. Yea, and Alexander's holy water yet at this day remaineth in England, and is used for a remedy against spirits and to chase away devils; yea, and I would this had been the worst. I would this were the worst. But wo worth thee, O devil, that hast prevailed to evacuate Christ's cross, and to mingle the Lord's supper. These be the Italian bishop's devices, and the devil hath pricked at this mark to frustrate the cross of Christ: he shot at this mark long before Christ came, he shot at it four thousand years before Christ hanged on the cross, or suffered His passion.

For the brasen serpent was set up in the wilderness, to put men in remembrance of Christ's coming; that like as they which beheld the brasen serpent were healed of their bodily diseases, so they that looked spiritually upon Christ that was to come, in Him should be saved spiritually from the devil. The serpent was set up in memory of Christ to come; but the devil found means to steal away the memory of Christ's coming, and

[1] Alexander I.

brought the people to worship the serpent itself, and to cense him, to honour him, and to offer to him, to worship him, and to make an idol of him. And this was done by the market-men that I told you of. And the clerk of the market did it for the lucre and advantage of his master, that thereby his honour might increase; for by Christ's death he could have but small worldly advantage.

And so even now so hath he certain blanchers belonging to the market, to let and stop the light of the gospel, and to hinder the king's proceedings in setting forth the word and glory of God. And when the king's majesty, with the advice of his honourable council, goeth about to promote God's word, and to set an order in matters of religion, there shall not lack blanchers that will say, ' As for images, whereas they have used to be censed, and to have candles offered unto them, none be so foolish to do it to the stock or stone, or to the image itself; but it is done to God and his honour before the image.' And though they should abuse it, these blanchers will be ready to whisper the king in the ear, and to tell him, that this abuse is but a small matter; and that the same, with all other like abuses in the church, may be reformed easily. ' It is but a little abuse,' say they, ' and it may be easily amended. But it should not be taken in hand at the first, for fear of trouble or further inconveniences. The people will not bear sudden alterations; an

H

insurrection may be made after sudden mutation, which may be to the great harm and loss of the realm. Therefore all things shall be well, but not out of hand, for fear of further business.'

These be the blanchers, that hitherto have stopped the word of God, and hindered the true setting forth of the same. There be so many put-offs, so many put-byes, so many respects and considerations of worldly wisdom : and I doubt not but there were blanchers in the old time to whisper in the ear of good king Hezekiah, for the maintenance of idolatry done to the brasen serpent, as well as there hath been now of late, and be now, that can blanch the abuse of images, and other like things. But good king Hezekiah would not be so blinded ; he was like to Apollos, 'fervent in spirit.' He would give no ear to the blanchers ; he was not moved with the worldly respects, with these prudent considerations, with these policies : he feared not insurrections of the people : he feared not lest his people would not bear the glory of God ; but he, without any of these respects, or policies, or considerations, like a good king, for God's sake and for conscience sake, by and by plucked down the brasen serpent, and destroyed it utterly, and beat it to powder. He out of hand did cast out all images, he destroyed all idolatry, and clearly did extirpate all superstition. He would not hear these blanchers and worldly-wise men, but without delay followeth

God's cause, and destroyeth all idolatry out of hand. Thus did good king Hezekiah; for he was like Apollos, fervent in spirit, and diligent to promote God's glory.

And good hope there is, that it shall be likewise here in England; for the king's majesty[1] is so brought up in knowledge, virtue, and godliness, that it is not to be mistrusted but that we shall have all things well, and that the glory of God shall be spread abroad throughout all parts of the realm, if the prelates will diligently apply their plough, and be preachers rather than lords. But our blanchers, which will be lords, and no labourers, when they are commanded to go and be resident upon their cures, and preach in their benefices, they would say, 'What? I have set a deputy there; I have a deputy that looketh well to my flock, and the which shall discharge my duty.' 'A deputy,' quoth he! I looked for that word all this while. And what a deputy must he be, trow ye? Even one like himself: he must be a canonist; that is to say, one that is brought up in the study of the pope's laws and decrees; one that will set forth papistry as well as himself will do; and one that will maintain all superstition and idolatry; and one that will nothing at all, or else very weakly, resist the devil's plough: yea, happy it is if he take no part with the devil; and

---

[1] Edward VI. had succeeded to the throne on January 28, 1547, a year before the delivery of this sermon.

where he should be an enemy to him, it is well if he take not the devil's part against Christ.

But in the mean time the prelates take their pleasures. They are lords, and no labourers: but the devil is diligent at his plough. He is no unpreaching prelate; he is no lordly loiterer from his cure, but a busy ploughman; so that among all the prelates, and among all the pack of them that have cure, the devil shall go for my money, for he still applieth his business. Therefore, ye unpreaching prelates, learn of the devil: to be diligent in doing of your office, learn of the devil: and if you will not learn of God, nor good men, for shame learn of the devil; *ad erubescentiam vestram dico*, 'I speak it for your shame': if you will not learn of God, nor good men, to be diligent in your office, learn of the devil. Howbeit there is now very good hope that the king's majesty, being by the help of good governance of his most honourable counsellors trained and brought up in learning, and knowledge of God's word, will shortly provide a remedy, and set an order herein; which thing that it may so be, let us pray for him. Pray for him, good people; pray for him. Ye have great cause and need to pray for him.

THE PASSION OF CHRIST.[1]

Romans xv. 4.—'Whatsoever things were written aforetime.' . . .

By occasion of this text, most honourable
audience, I have walked this Lent in the broad
field of scripture, and used my liberty, and entreated of such matters as I thought meet for this
auditory. I have had ado with many estates,
even with the highest of all. I have entreated
of the duty of kings, of the duty of magistrates
and judges, of the duty of prelates; allowing
that that is good, and disallowing the contrary.
I have taught that we are all sinners: I think
there is none of us all, neither preacher nor
hearer, but we may be amended, and redress our
lives: we may all say, yea, all the pack of us,
Peccavimus cum patribus nostris, 'We have
offended and sinned with our forefathers.'[2] *In
multis offendimus omnes:* there is none of us all
but we have in sundry things grievously offended
almighty God. I here entreated of many faults,

[1] The Seventh Sermon before King Edward VI., preached on
Good Friday, April 19, 1549.
[2] Ps. cvi. 6.

and rebuked many kinds of sins. I intend to-day, by God's grace, to shew you the remedy of sin. We be in the place of repentance : now is the time to call for mercy, whilst we be in this world. We be all sinners, even the best of us all ; therefore it is good to hear the remedy of sin. This day is commonly called Good Friday : although every day ought to be with us Good Friday, yet this day we are accustomed specially to have a commemoration and remembrance of the passion of our Saviour Jesus Christ. This day we have in memory his bitter passion and death, which is the remedy of our sin. Therefore I intend to entreat of a piece of a story of his passion ; I am not able to entreat of all. That I may do that the better, and that it may be to the honour of God, and the edification of your souls, and mine both, I shall desire you to pray, etc. In this prayer I will desire you to remember the souls departed, with lauds and praise to almighty God, and that he did vouchsafe to assist them at the hour of their death : in so doing you shall be put in remembrance to pray for yourselves, that it may please God to assist and comfort you in the agonies and pains of death.

The place that I will entreat of is the twenty-sixth chapter of St Matthew. Howbeit, as I entreat of it, I will borrow part of St Mark,[1] and part of St Luke[2] : for they have somewhat that

---

[1] Luke xxii.   [2] Mark xiv.

St Matthew hath not; and especially Luke. The text is, *Tunc cum venisset Jesus in villam, quæ dicitur Gethsemani*, 'Then when Jesus came;' some have *in villam*, some *in agrum*, some *in prædium*. But it is all one; when Christ came into a grange, into a piece of land, into a field, it makes no matter; call it what ye will. At what time He had come into an honest man's house, and there eaten His paschal lamb, and instituted and celebrated the Lord's supper, and set forth the blessed communion; then, when this was done, He took his way to the place where He knew Judas would come. It was a solitary place, and thither He went with His eleven apostles: for Judas, the twelfth, was about his business, he was occupied about his merchandise, and was providing among the bishops and priests to come with an ambushment of Jews to take our Saviour Jesus Christ. And when He was come into the field or grange, this village or farm-place, which was called Gethsemane, there was a garden, saith Luke, into the which He goeth, and leaves eight of His disciples without; howbeit He appointed them what they should do: He saith, *Sedete hic donec illuc vadam et orem;* 'Sit you here, whilst I go yonder and pray.' He told them that He went to pray, to monish them what they should do, to fall to prayer as He did. He left them there, and took no more with Him but three, Peter, James, and John, to teach us that a solitary

place is meet for prayer. Then when He was
come into this garden, *cœpit expavescere*, 'He
began to tremble,' insomuch He said, *Tristis est
anima mea usque ad mortem,* 'My soul is heavy
and pensive even unto death.'

This is a notable place, and one of the most
especial and chiefest of all that be in the story of
the passion of Christ. Here is our remedy: here
we must have in consideration all His doings and
sayings, for our learning, for our edification, for
our comfort and consolation.

First of all, He set His three disciples that He
took with Him in an order, and told them what
they should do, saying, *Sedete hic, et vigilate
mecum, et orate;* 'Sit here, and pray that ye
enter not into temptation.' But of that I will
entreat afterward. Now when He was in the
garden, *Cœpit expavescere*, He began to be heavy,
pensive, heavy-hearted. I like not Origen's playing with this word *cœpit*; it was a perfect heaviness; it was such a one as was never seen a
greater; it was not only the beginning of a
sorrow. These doctors, we have great cause to
thank God for them, but yet I would not have
them always to be allowed. They have handled
many points of our faith very godly; and we
may have a great stay in them in many
things; we might not well lack them: but yet
I would not have men to be sworn to them, and
so addict, as to take hand over head whatsoever

they say: it were a great inconvenience so to do.

Well, let us go forward. He took Peter, James, and John, into this garden. And why did He take them with Him rather than other? Marry, those that He had taken before, to whom He had revealed in the hill the transfiguration and declaration of His deity, to see the revelation of the majesty of His Godhead, now in the garden He revealed to the same the infirmity of His manhood: because they had tasted of the sweet He would they should taste also of the sour. He took these with Him at both times: for two or three is enough to bear witness. And He began to be heavy in His mind; He was greatly vexed within Himself, He was sore afflicted, it was a great heaviness. He had been heavy many times before; and He had suffered great afflictions in His soul, as for the blindness of the Jews; and He was like to suffer more pangs of pain in His body. But this pang was greater than any that He ever suffered: yea, it was a greater torment unto Him, I think a greater pain, than when He was hanged on the cross; than when the four nails were knocked and driven through His hands and feet; than when the sharp crown of thorns was thrust on His head. This was the heaviness and pensiveness of His heart, the agony of the spirit. And as the soul is more precious than the body, even so is the pains of the soul more grievous than the pains of the body : therefore there is another which writeth, *Horror mortis gravior ipsa morte ;* ' The horror and ugsomeness of death is sorer than death itself.' This is the most grievous pain that ever Christ suffered, even this pang that He suffered in the garden. It is the most notable place, one of them in the whole story of the passion, when He said, *Anima mea tristis est usque ad mortem,* ' My soul is heavy to death ; ' and *cum cœpisset expavescere,* ' when He began to quiver, to shake.' The grievousness of it is declared by this prayer that He made : *Pater, si possibile est,* etc., ' Father, if it be possible, away with this cup : rid me of it.' He understood by this cup His pains of death ; for He knew well enough that His passion was at hand, that Judas was coming upon Him with the Jews to take Him.

There was offered unto Him now the image of death ; the image, the sense, the feeling of hell : for death and hell go both together. I will entreat of this image of hell, which is death. Truly no man can show it perfectly, yet I will do the best I can to make you understand the grievous pangs that our Saviour Christ was in when He was in the garden. As man's power is not able to bear it, so no man's tongue is able to express it. Painters paint death like a man without skin, and a body having nothing but bones. And hell they paint with horrible flames of burning fire : they bungle somewhat at it, they come nothing near it. But this is no true painting. No painter can paint hell, unless he could paint the torment and condemnation both of body and soul ; the possession and having of all infelicity. This is hell, this is the image of death : this is hell, such an evil-favoured face, such an uglesome countenance, such an horrible visage our Saviour Christ saw of death and hell in the garden. There is no pleasure in beholding of it, but more pain than any tongue can tell. Death and hell took unto them this evil-favoured face of sin, and through sin. This sin is so highly hated of God, that He doth pronounce it worthy to be punished with lack of all felicity, with the feeling of infelicity. Death and hell be not only the wages, the reward, the stipend of sin : but they are brought into the world by sin. *Per peccatum mors*, saith St Paul, 'through sin death entered into the world.' [1] Moses sheweth the first coming in of it into the world.' Whereas as our first father Adam was set at liberty to live for ever, yet God inhibiting him from eating of the apple, told him : "If thou meddle with this fruit, thou and all thy posterity shall fall into necessity of death, from ever living : *moter morieris*, thou and all thy posterity shall be subject to death.' [2] Here came in death and hell : sin was their mother ; therefore they must

---

[1] Romans v. 12.   [2] Gen. 2 17.

have such an image as their mother sin would
give them.

An uglesome thing and an horrible image must
it needs be, that is brought in by such a thing so
hated of God ; yea, this face of death and hell is
so terrible, that such as have been wicked men
had rather be hanged than abide it. As
Achitophel, that traitor to David, like an
ambitious wretch, thought to have come to
higher promotion, and therefore conspired with
Absolon against his master David : he, when he
saw his counsel took no place, goes and hangs
himself, in contemplation of this evil-favoured face
of death. Judas also, when he came with bush-
ments to take his master Christ, in beholding this
horrible face, hanged himself. Yea, the elect
people of God, the faithful, having the beholding
of His face (though God hath always preserved
them, such a good God He is to them that
believe in Him, that ' He will not suffer them to
be tempted above that that they have been able to
bear,' [1] yet for all that, there is nothing that they
complain more sore than of this horror of death.
Go to Job, what saith he? *Pereat dies in quo
natus sum suspendium elegit anima mea;* ' Wo worth
the day that I was born in, my soul would be
hanged ; ' [2] saying in his pangs almost he wist not
what. This was when with the eye of his conscience and the inward man he beheld the horror

---

[1] 1 Cor. x. 13.   [2] Job iii. 3.

of death and hell : not for any bodily pain he
suffered ; for when he had boils, blotches, blains,
and scabs, he suffered them patiently : he could
say then, *Si bona suscepi de manu Domini,* etc., ' If
we have received good things of God, why should
we not suffer likewise evil ' ? [1] It was not for any
such thing that he was so vexed : but the sight of
this face of death and hell was offered to him so
lively, that he would have been out of this world.
It was this evil-favoured face of death that so
troubled him.

King David also said, in contemplation of this
uglesome face, *Laboravi in gemitu meo,* ' I have
been sore vexed with sighing and mourning.'
Turbatus est a furore oculus meus, ' Mine eye hath
been greatly troubled in my rage.' [2] A strange
thing ! When he had to fight with Goliath, that
monstrous giant, who was able to have eaten him,
he could abide him, and was nothing afraid. And
now what a work ! What exclamations makes he
at the sight of death ! Jonas likewise was bold
enough to bid the shipmen cast him into the sea,
he had not seen that face and visage : but when
he was in the whale's belly, and had there the
beholding of it, what terror and distress abode he !
Hezekiah, when he saw Sennacherib besieging his
city on every side most violently, was nothing
afraid of the great host and mighty army that
was like to destroy him out of hand ; yet he was

[1] Job ii. 10.   [2] Ps. xxxi. 9, 10.

afraid of death. When the prophet came unto
him and said, *Dispone domui tuæ, morte morieris et
non vives*, 'Set thy house in order, for thou shalt
surely die, and not live' (2 Kings xx.), it struck
him so to the heart that he fell a-weeping. O
Lord, what an horror was this!   There be some
writers that say, that Peter, James, and John were
in this feeling at the same time ; and that Peter,
when he said, *Exi a me, Domine, quia homo peccator
sum*, 'Depart from me, O Lord, for I am a sinful
man,'[1] did taste some part of it : he was so
astonished, he wist not what to say.   It was not
long that they were in this anguish ; some say
longer, some shorter : but Christ was ready to
comfort them, and said to Peter, *Ne timeas*, 'Be
not afraid.'   A friend of mine told me of a certain
woman that was eighteen years together in it.
I knew a man myself, Bilney,[2] little Bilney, that
blessed martyr of God, what time he had borne
his fagot,[3] and was come again to Cambridge, had
such conflicts within himself, beholding this image
of death, that his friends were afraid to let him be
alone : they were fain to be with him day and
night, and comforted him as they could, but no
comforts would serve. As for the comfortable
places of scripture, to bring them unto him it was

[1] Luke v. 8.

[2] Burned at Norwich, August 19, 1531.

[3] Bilney had recanted his Protestant opinions, and on December
8, 1527, had stood bearing a faggot whilst a preacher exulted over
his return to the fold.

as though a man would run him through the heart with a sword; yet afterward, for all this, he was revived, and took his death patiently, and died well against the tyrannical see of Rome.[1] Wo will be to that bishop that had the examination of him, if he repented not!

Here is a good lesson for you, my friends; if ever you come in danger, in durance, in prison for God's quarrel, and His sake, as He did for purgatory-matters, and put to bear a fagot for preaching the true word of God against pilgrimage, and such like matters, I will advise you first, and above all things, to abjure all your friends, all your friendships; leave not one unabjured. It is they that shall undo you, and not your enemies. It was his very friends that brought Bilney to it.

By this it may somewhat appear what our Saviour Christ suffered; He doth not dissemble it Himself, when He saith, 'My soul is heavy to death,': He was in so sore an agony, that there issued out of Him, as I shall entreat anon, drops of blood. An ugsome thing surely, which this fact and deed sheweth us, what horrible pains He was in, for our sakes! But you will say, 'How can this be? It were possible that I, and such other as be great sinners, should suffer such affliction; the Son of God, what our Saviour Christ, [who] never sinned, how can this stand

[1] For the charge that Bilney died a Romanist, see Demaus's *Hugh Latimer*, pp. 130, 131.

that He should be thus handled ? He never deserved it.'

Marry, I will tell you how. We must consider our Saviour Christ two ways, one way in His manhood, another in His Godhead. Some places of scripture must be referred to His Deity, and some to His humanity. In His Godhead He suffered nothing ; but now He made Himself void of His Deity, as scripture saith, *Cum esset in forma Dei, exinanivit seipsum*, 'Whereas He was in the form of God, He emptied Himself of it, He did hide it, and used Himself as though He had not had it.'[1] He would not help Himself with His Godhead ; 'He humbled Himself with all obedience unto death, even to the death of the cross :' this was in that He was man. He took upon Him our sins :[2] not the work of sin ; I mean not so : not to do it, not to commit it ; but to purge it, to cleanse it, to bear the stipend of it : and that way He was the great sinner of the world. He bare all the sin of the world on His back ; He would become debtor for it.

Now to sustain and suffer the dolours of death is not to sin : but He came into this world with His passion to purge our sins. Now this that He suffered in the garden is one of the bitterest pieces of all His passion : this fear of death was the bitterest pain that ever He abode, due to sin which He never did, but became debtor for us.

[1] Phil. ii. 617. [2] Isa. liii. 6.

All this He suffered for us ; this He did to satisfy
for our sins. It is much like as if I owed another
man twenty thousand pounds, and should pay it
out of hand, or else go to the dungeon of Ludgate[1];
and when I am going to prison, one of my friends
should come, and ask, ' Whither goeth this man ? '
and after he had heard the matter, should say,
' Let me answer for him, I will become surety for
him : yea, I will pay all for him.' Such a part
played our Saviour Christ with us. If He had not
suffered this, I for my part should have suffered,
according to the gravity and quantity of my sins,
damnation. For the greater the sin is, the greater
is the punishment in hell. He suffered for you
and me, in such a degree as is due to all the sins
of the whole world. It was as if you would
imagine that one man had committed all the sins
since Adam : you may be sure he should be
punished with the same horror of death, in such
a sort as all men in the world should have
suffered.

Feign and put case, our Saviour Christ had
committed all the sins of the world ; all that I
for my part have done, all that you for your part
have done, and that any man else hath done : if
He had done all this Himself, His agony that
He suffered should have been no greater nor
grievouser than it was. This that He suffered
in the garden was a portion, I say, of His passion,

---

[1] A debtors' prison.

I

and one of the bitterest parts of it.   And this He
suffered for our sins, and not for any sins that He
had committed Himself : for all we should have
suffered, every man according to his own deserts.
This He did of His goodness, partly to purge
and cleanse our sins, partly because He would
taste and feel our miseries, *quo possit succurrere
nobis,* 'that He should the rather help and relieve
us ;' and partly He suffered to give us example
to behave ourselves as He did. He did not suffer,
to discharge us clean from death, to keep us clean
from it, not to taste of it.   Nay, nay, you must
not take it so. We shall have the beholding of
this ugsome face every one of us ; we shall feel it
ourselves.   Yet our Saviour Christ did suffer, to
the intent to signify to us that death is overcome-
able. We shall indeed overcome it, if we repent,
and acknowledge that our Saviour Jesu Christ
pacified with His pangs and pains the wrath of
the Father ; having a love to walk in the ways of
God.   If we believe in Jesu Christ, we shall overcome death : I say it shall not prevail against us.
Wherefore, whensoever it chanceth thee, my friend,
to have the tasting of this death, that thou shalt
be tempted with this horror of death, what is to
be done then ? Whensoever thou feelest thy soul
heavy to death, make haste and resort to this
garden ; and with this faith thou shalt overcome
this terror when it cometh. Oh, it was a grievous
thing that Christ suffered here !   O the greatness

of this dolour that He suffered in the garden,
partly to make amends for our sins, and partly
to deliver us from death ; not so that we should
not die bodily, but that this death should be a
way to a better life, and to destroy and overcome
hell ! Our Saviour Christ had a garden, but He
had little pleasure in it. You have many goodly
gardens : I would you would in the midst of them
consider what agony our Saviour Christ suffered
in His garden. A goodly meditation to have in
your gardens ! It shall occasion you to delight
no farther in vanities, but to remember what He
suffered for you. It may draw you from sin.
It is a good monument, a good sign, a good
monition, to consider how He behaved Himself
in this garden.

Well ; He saith to His disciples, ' Sit here and
pray with Me.' He went a little way off, as it
were a stone's cast from them, and falleth to His
prayer, and saith : *Pater, si possibile est, transeat a
me calix iste ;* ' Father, if it be possible, away with
this bitter cup, this outrageous pain.' Yet after
He corrects Himself, and says, *Veruntamen non
sicut ego volo, sed sicut tu vis ;* ' Not My will, but
Thy will be done, O Father.' Here is a good
meditation for christian men at all times, and not
only upon Good Friday. Let Good Friday be
every day to a christian man, to know to use his
passion to that end and purpose ; not only to read
the story, but to take the fruit of it. Some men,

if they had been in this agony, would have run themselves through with their swords, as Saul did : some would have hanged themselves, as Achitophel did. Let us not follow these men, they be no examples for us ; but let us follow Christ, which in His agony resorted to His Father with His prayer. This must be our pattern to work by.

Here I might dilate the matter as touching praying to saints. Here we may learn not to pray to saints. Christ bids us, *Ora Patrem qui est in cœlis*, ' Pray to thy Father that is in heaven ; ' to the Creator, and not to any creature. And therefore away with these avowries [1] : let God alone be our avowry. What have we to do to run hither or thither, but only to the Father of heaven ? I will not tarry to speak of this matter.

Our Saviour Christ set His disciples in an order, and commanded them to watch and pray, saying, *Vigilate et orate ;* ' Watch and pray.' Whereto should they watch and pray ? He saith by and by, *ne intretis in tentationem*, ' that ye enter not into temptation.' He bids them not pray that we be not tempted ; for that is as much to say, as to pray that we should be out of this world. There is no man in this world without temptation. In the time of prosperity we are tempted to wantonness, pleasures, and all lightness ; in time of adversity, to despair in God's goodness. Temptation never ceases. There is a

---

[1] Avowries, protectors.

difference between being tempted, and entering into temptation. He bids therefore not to pray that they be not tempted, but that they 'enter not into temptation.' To be tempted is no evil thing. For what is it? No more than when the flesh, the devil and the world, doth solicit and move us against God. To give place to these suggestions, and to yield ourselves, and suffer us to be overcome of them, this is to enter into temptation. Our Saviour Christ knew that they should be grievously tempted, and therefore He gave them warning that they should not give place to temptation, nor despair at His death: and if they chanced to forsake Him, or to run away, in case they tripped or swerved, yet to come again.

But our Saviour Christ did not only command His disciples to pray, but fell down upon His knees flat upon the ground, and prayed Himself, saying, *Pater, si fieri potest, transeat a me calix iste;* 'Father, deliver Me of this pang and pain that I am in, this outrageous pain.' This word, 'Father,' came even from the bowels of His heart, when He made His moan; as who should say, 'Father, rid Me; I am in such pain that I can be in no greater! Thou art My Father, I am Thy Son. Can the Father forsake His Son in such anguish?' Thus He made His moan. 'Father, take away this horror of death from Me; rid Me of this pain; suffer Me not to be taken when

Judas comes; suffer Me not to be hanged on the cross; suffer not My hands to be pierced with nails, nor My heart with the sharp spear.' A wonderful thing, that He should so oft tell His disciples of it before, and now, when He cometh to the point, to desire to be rid of it, as though He would have been disobedient to the will of His Father. Afore He said, He came to suffer; and now He says, away with this cup. Who would have thought that ever this gear should have come out of Christ's mouth? What a case is this! What should a man say? You must understand, that Christ took upon Him our infirmities, of the which this was one, to be sorry at death. Among the stipends of sin, this was one, to tremble at the cross: this is a punishment for our sin.

It goeth otherways with us than with Christ: if we were in like case, and in like agony, almost we would curse God, or rather wish that there were no God. This that He said was not of that sort; it was referring the matter to the will of His Father. But we seek by all means, be it right, be it wrong, of our own nature to be rid out of pain: he desired it conditionally, as it might stand with His Father's will; adding a *veruntamen* to it. So His request was to shew the infirmity of man. Here is now an example what we shall do when we are in like case. He never deserved it, we have. He had a *veruntamen*,

and notwithstanding : let us have so too. We
must have a 'nevertheless, Thy will be done, and
not mine : give me grace to be content, to submit
my will unto Thine.' His fact teacheth us what
to do. This is our surgery, our physic, when
we be in agony : and reckon upon it, friends,
we shall come to it ; we shall feel it at one
time or another.

What doth He now ? What came to pass
now, when He had heard no voice, His Father
was dumb ? He resorts to His friends, seeking
some comfort at their hands. Seeing He had
none at His Father's hand, He cometh to His
disciples, and finds them asleep. He spake unto
Peter, and said, 'Ah Peter, art thou asleep ?'
Peter before had bragged stoutly, as though he
would have killed, (God have mercy upon his
soul !) and now, when he should have comforted
Christ, he was asleep. Not once buff nor baff
to him : not a word. He was fain to say to
His disciples, *Vigilate et orate*, 'Watch and pray ;
the spirit is ready, but the flesh is weak :' He
had never a word of them again. They might
at the least have said, 'O Sir, remember Yourself ; are You not Christ ? Came not You into
this world to redeem sin ? Be of good cheer,
be of good comfort : this sorrow will not help
You ; comfort Yourself by Your own preaching.
You have said, *Oportet Filium hominis pati*, 'It
behoveth the Son of man to suffer.' You have

not deserved any thing, it is not Your fault.'
Indeed, if they had done this with Him, they
had played a friendly part with Him; but they
gave Him not so much as one comfortable word.
We run to our friends in our distresses and
agonies, as though we had all our trust and
confidence in them. He did not so; He resorted
to them, but trusted not in them. We will run
to our friends, and come no more to God; He
returned again. What! Shall we not resort to
our friends in time of need? And, trow ye, we
shall not find them asleep? Yes, I warrant you:
and when we need their help most, we shall not
have it. But what shall we do, when we shall
find lack in them? We will cry out upon them,
upbraid them, chide, brawl, fume, chafe, and back-
bite them. But Christ did not so; He excused
His friends, saying, *Vigilate et orate; spiritus
quidem promptus est, caro autem infirma:* 'O!'
quoth He, 'watch and pray: I see well the
spirit is ready, but the flesh is weak.' What
meaneth this? Surely it is a comfortable place.
For as long as we live in this world, when we
be at the best, we have no more but *promptitu-
dinem spiritus cum infirmitate carnis*, the readiness
of the spirit with the infirmity of the flesh. The
very saints of God said, *Velle adest mihi*, 'My
will is good, but I am not able to perform it.'[1]
I have been with some, and fain they would, fain

[1] Rom. vii. 18.

they would : there was readiness of spirit, but it
would not be ; it grieved them that they could
not take things as they should do. The flesh
resisteth the work of the Holy Ghost in our
hearts, and lets it, lets it. We have to pray
ever to God. O prayer, prayer! that it might
be used in this realm, as it ought to be of all
men, and specially of magistrates, of counsellors,
of great rulers ; to pray, to pray that it would
please God to put godly policies in their hearts!
Call for assistance.

I have heard say, when that good queen[1] that
is gone had ordained in her house daily prayer
both before noon, and after noon, the admiral
gets him out of the way, like a mole digging
in the earth. He shall be Lot's wife to me as
long as I live. He was, I heard say, a covetous
man, a covetous man indeed : I would there were
no more in England! He was, I heard say, an
ambitious man : I would there were no more in
England! He was, I heard say, a seditious man,
a contemner of common prayer : I would there
were no more in England! Well : he is gone.[2]
I would he had left none behind him ! Remember
you, my lords, that you pray in your houses to

[1] Catherine Parr, who, after the death of Henry VIII., married
the lord admiral Seymour.

[2] Seymour was convicted of high treason and executed on
March 20, 1549, a month before the delivery of this sermon.
Seymour was of an overbearing disposition, and Latimer seems
to have thought him a profligate also.

the better mortification of your flesh. Remember God must be honoured. I will you to pray, that God will continue His Spirit in you. I do not put you in comfort, that if ye have once the Spirit, ye cannot lose it. There be new spirits start up now of late, that say, after we have received the Spirit, we cannot sin. I will make but one argument: St Paul had brought the Galatians to the profession of the faith, and left them in that state; they had received the Spirit once, but they sinned again, as he testified of them himself: he saith, *Currebatis bene;* [1] ye were once in a right state: and again, *Recepistis Spiritum ex operibus legis an ex justitia fidei?* [2] Once they had the Spirit by faith; but false prophets came, when he was gone from them, and they plucked them clean away from all that Paul had planted them in: and then said Paul unto them, *O stulti Galati, quis vos fascinavit?* 'O foolish Galatians, who hath bewitched you?' [3] If this be true, we may lose the Spirit that we have once possessed. It is a fond thing: I will not tarry in it. But now to the passion again.

Christ had been with His Father, and felt no help: He had been with His friends, and had no comfort: He had prayed twice, and was not heard: what did He now? Did He give prayer over? No, He goeth again to His Father, and saith the same again: 'Father, if it be possible,

[1] Gal. v. 7.   [2] Gal. iii. 2.   [3] Gal. iii. 1.

away with this cup.'[1] Here is an example for
us, although we be not heard at the first time,
shall we give over our prayer? Nay, we must
to it again. [We must be importune upon God.]
We must be instant in prayer. He prayed thrice,
and was not heard ; let us pray threescore times.
Folks are very dull now-a-days in prayer, to come
to sermons, to resort to common prayer. You
house-keepers, and especially great men, give
example of prayer in your houses.

Well ; did His Father look upon Him this
second time? No, He went to His friends again,
thinking to find some comfort there, but He finds
them asleep again ; more deep asleep than ever
they were : their eyes were heavy with sleep ;
there was no comfort at all ; they wist not what
to say to Him. A wonderful thing, how he was
tost from post to pillar ; one while to His Father,
and was destitute at His hand ; another while to
His friends, and found no comfort at them : His
Father gave Him looking on, and suffered Him
to bite upon the bridle awhile. Almighty God
beheld this battle, that He might enjoy the honour
and glory ; 'that in His name all knees should
bow, *cœlestium, terrestrium et infernorum*, in
heaven, earth, and hell.' This, that the Father
would not hear His own Son, was another punishment due to our sin. When we cry unto Him,
He will not hear us. The prophet Jeremy saith,

[1] Matt. xx. 39.

Clamabunt ad me et ego non exaudiam eos; ' They shall cry unto Me, and I will not hear them.'[1] These be Jeremy's words : here he threateneth to punish sin with not hearing their prayers. The prophet saith, ' They have not had the fear of God before their eyes, nor have not regarded discipline and correction.'[2] I never saw, surely, so little discipline as is now-a-days. Men will be masters ; they will be masters and no disciples.

Alas, where is this discipline now in England ? The people regard no discipline ; they be without all order. Where they should give place, they will not stir one inch : yea, where magistrates should determine matters, they will break into the place before they come, and at their coming not move a whit for them. Is this discipline ? Is this good order ? If a man say anything unto them, they regard it not. They that be called to answer, will not answer directly, but scoff the matter out. Men the more they know, the worse they be ; it is truly said, *scientia inflat,* ' knowledge maketh us proud, and causeth us to forget all, and set away discipline.' Surely in popery they had a reverence ; but now we have none at all. I never saw the like. This same lack of the fear of God and discipline in us was one of the causes that the Father would not hear His Son. This pain suffered our Saviour Christ for us, who never deserved it. O, what

[1] Jer. xi. 14.   [2] Jer. vii. 28.

it was that He suffered in this garden, till Judas
came! The dolours, the terrors, the sorrows that
He suffered be unspeakable! He suffered partly
to make amends for our sins, and partly to give
us example, what we should do in like case.
What comes of this gear in the end?

Well; now He prayeth again, He resorteth to
His Father again. *Angore correptus prolixius
orabat:* He was in sorer pains, in more anguish
than ever He was; and therefore He prayeth
longer, more ardently, more fervently, more
vehemently, than ever He did before. O Lord,
what a wonderful thing is this! This horror of
death is worse than death itself, and is more
ugsome. He prayeth now the third time. He
did it so instantly, so fervently, that it brought
out a bloody sweat, and in such plenty, that it
dropped down even to the ground. There issued
out of His precious body drops of blood. What
a pain was He in, when these bloody drops fell so
abundantly from Him! Yet for all that, how
unthankful do we shew ourselves toward Him that
died only for our sakes, and for the remedy of our
sins! O what blasphemy do we commit day by
day! what little regard have we to His blessed
passion, thus to swear by God's blood, by Christ's
passion! We have nothing in our pastime, but
'God's blood,' 'God's wounds.' We continually
blaspheme His passion, in hawking, hunting,
dicing, and carding. Who would think He

should have such enemies among those that profess His name? What became of His blood that fell down, trow ye? Was the blood of Hales [1] of it? Wo worth it! What ado was there to bring this out of the king's [2] head! This great abomination, of the blood of Hales, could not be taken a great while out of his mind.

You that be of the court, and especially ye sworn chaplains, beware of a lesson that a great man taught me at my first coming to the court: he told me for good-will; he thought it well. He said to me, 'You must beware, howsoever ye do, that ye contrary not the king; let him have his sayings; follow him; go with him.' Marry, out upon this counsel! Shall I say as he says? Say your conscience, or else what a worm shall ye feel gnawing; what a remorse of conscience shall ye have, when ye remember how ye have slacked your duty! It is a good wise verse, *Gutta cavat lapidem non vi sed sæpe cadendo;* 'The drop of rain maketh a hole in the stone, not by violence, but by oft falling.' Likewise a prince must be turned; not violently, but he must be won by a little and a little. He must have his duty told him; but it must be done with humbleness, with

---

[1] A relic, kept in the Abbey of Hales in Gloucestershire. It was said to be a portion of our Saviour's blood brought from Jerusalem, but when examined it was found to be coloured honey. Latimer himself investigated and exposed the fraud. See Demaus's *Hugh Latimer*, pp. 316-18. Ed. 1904.

[2] King Henry VIII

request of pardon ; or else it were a dangerous thing. Unpreaching prelates have been the cause, that the blood of Hales did so long blind the king. Wo worth that such an abominable thing should be in a christian realm ! But thanks be to God, it was partly redressed in the king's days that dead is, and much more now. God grant good-will and power to go forward, if there be any such abomination behind, that it may be utterly rooted up !

O how happy are we, that it hath pleased Almighty God to vouchsafe that His Son should sweat blood for the redeeming of our sins ! And, again, how unhappy are we, if we will not take it thankfully, that were redeemed so painfully ! Alas, what hard hearts have we ! Our Saviour Christ never sinned, and yet sweat He blood for our sins. We will not once water our eyes with a few tears. What an horrible thing is sin ; that no other thing would remedy and pay the ransom for it, but only the blood of our Saviour Christ ! There was nothing to pacify the Father's wrath against man, but such an agony as He suffered. All the passion of all the martyrs that ever were, all the sacrifices of patriarchs that ever were, all the good works that ever were done, were not able to remedy our sin, to make satisfaction for our sins, nor anything besides, but this extreme passion and bloodshedding of our most merciful Saviour Christ.

But to draw toward an end.   What became of this threefold prayer?   At the length, it pleased God to hear His Son's prayer; and sent Him an angel to corroborate, to strengthen, to comfort Him.   Christ needed no angel's help, if He had listed to ease Himself with His deity.   He was the Son of God : what then?   Forsomuch as He was man, He received comfort at the angel's hand ; as it accords to our infirmity.   His obedience, His continuance, and suffering, so pleased the Father of heaven, that for His Son's sake, be he never so great a sinner, leaving his sin, and repenting for the same, he will owe him such favour as though he had never committed any sin.   The Father of heaven will not suffer him to be tempted with this great horror of death and hell to the utter-most, and above that he is able to bear.   Look for it, my friends, by Him and through Him, we shall be able to overcome it.   Let us do as our Saviour Christ did, and we shall have help from above, we shall have angels' help : if we trust in Him, heaven and earth shall give up, rather than we shall lack help.   He saith He is *Adjutor in necessitatibus*, ' an helper in time of need.'

When the angel had comforted Him, and when this horror of death was gone, He was so strong that He offered Himself to Judas ; and said, ' I am He.'   To make an end : I pray you take pains : it is a day of penance, as we use to say, give me leave to make you weary this day.   The

Jews had Him to Caiaphas and Annas, and there
they whipped Him, and beat Him : they set a
crown of sharp thorns upon His head, and nailed
Him to a tree : yet all this was not so bitter, as
this horror of death, and this agony that He
suffered in the garden, in such a degree as is due
to all the sins of the world, and not to one man's
sins.   Well ; this passion is our remedy ; it is
the satisfaction for our sins.

His soul descended to hell for a time.   Here is
much ado !   These new upstarting spirits say,
' Christ never descended into hell, neither body
nor soul.'   In scorn they will ask, ' Was He
there ?   What did He there ? '   What if we
cannot tell what He did there ?   The creed
goeth no further, but saith, He descended thither.
What is that to us, if we cannot tell, seeing we
were taught no further ?   Paul was taken up into
the third heaven ; ask likewise what he saw when
he was carried thither ?   You shall not find in
scripture, what he saw or what he did there :
shall we not, therefore, believe that he was there ?
These arrogant spirits, spirits of vain - glory,
because they know not by any express scripture
the order of His doings in hell, they will not
believe that ever He descended into hell.   Indeed
this article hath not so full scripture, so many
places and testimonies of scriptures, as others
have ; yet it hath enough : it hath two or three
texts ; and if it had but one, one text of scrip-

K

ture is of as good and lawful authority as a
thousand, and of as certain truth. It is not to be
weighed by the multitude of texts. I believe as
certainly and verily that this realm of England
hath as good authority to hear God's word, as
any nation in all the world : it may be gathered
by two texts : one of them is this : *Ite in univer-
sum mundum, et prædicate evangelium omni
creaturæ,* ' Go into the whole world, and preach
the gospel to all creatures.' [1]   Again, *Deus vult
omnes homines salvos fieri,* ' God will have all men
to be saved.' [2]   He excepts not the Englishmen
here, nor yet expressly nameth them ; and yet
I am as sure that this realm of England, by this
gathering, is allowed to hear God's word, as
though Christ had said a thousand times, ' Go
preach to Englishmen : I will that Englishmen
be saved.'   Because this article of His descending
into hell cannot be gathered so directly, so
necessarily, so formally, they utterly deny it.

This article hath scriptures two or three ;
enough for quiet minds : as for curious brains,
nothing can content them.   This the devil's
stirring up of such spirits of sedition is an evident
argument that the light is come forth ; for His
word is abroad when the devil rusheth, when he
roareth, when he stirreth up such busy spirits to
slander it.   My intent is not to entreat of this
matter at this time.   I trust the people will not be

----

[1] Mark xvi. 15.   [2] 1 Tim. ii. 4.

carried away with these new arrogant spirits. I doubt
not, but good preachers will labour against them.

But now I will say a word, and herein I pro-
test first of all, not arrogantly to determine and
define it : I will contend with no man for it ; I
will not have it to be prejudice to any body, but
I offer it unto you to consider and weigh it.
There be some great clerks that take my part, and
I perceive not what evil can come of it, in saying,
that our Saviour Christ did not only in soul descend
into hell, but also that He suffered in hell such
pains as the damned spirits did suffer there.
Surely, I believe verily, for my part, that He
suffered the pains of hell proportionably, as it
corresponds and answers to the whole sin of the
world. He would not suffer only bodily in the
garden and upon the cross, but also in his soul
when it was from the body ; which was a pain
due for our sin. Some write so, and I can believe
it, that He suffered in the very place, and I cannot
tell what it is, call it what you will, even in the
scalding-house, in the ugsomeness of the place, in
the presence of the place, such pain as our
capacity cannot attain unto : it is somewhat
declared unto us, when we utter it by these
effects, 'by fire, by gnashing of teeth, by the
worm that gnaweth on the conscience.' Whatsoever the pain is, it is a great pain that He
suffered for us.

I see no inconvenience to say, that Christ

suffered in soul in hell. I singularly commend
the exceeding great charity of Christ, that for our
sakes would suffer in hell in His soul. It sets
out the unspeakable hatred that God hath to sin.
I perceive not that it doth derogate anything from
the dignity of Christ's death ; as in the garden,
when He suffered, it derogates nothing from that
He suffered on the cross. Scripture speaketh on
this fashion : *Qui credit in me habet vitam æternam ;*[1]
'He that believeth in Me, hath life everlasting.'
Here He sets forth faith as the cause of our
justification ; in other places, as high commenda-
tion is given to works : and yet, are the works
any derogation from that dignity of faith ? No.

And again, scripture saith, *Traditus est propter
peccata nostra, et exsuscitatus propter justificationem,*[2]
&c. It attributeth here our justification to His
resurrection ; and doth this derogate anything
from His death ? Not a whit. It is whole Christ.
What with His nativity ; what with His circum-
cision ; what with His incarnation and the whole
process of His life ; with His preaching ; what
with His ascending, descending ; what with His
death ; it is all Christ that worketh our salvation.
He sitteth on the right hand of the Father, and
all for us. All this is the work of our salvation.
I would be as loth to derogate anything from
Christ's death, as the best of you all. How
inestimably are we bound to Him ! What thanks

---

[1] John vi. 47.   [2] Rom. iv. 25.

ought we to give Him for it! We must have
this continually in remembrance : *Propter te morti
tradimur tota die,* ' For Thee we are in dying continually.' The life of a Christian man is nothing
but a readiness to die, and a remembrance of death.

If this that I have spoken of Christ's suffering
in the garden, and in hell, derogate anything from
Christ's death and passion, away with it ; believe
me not in this. If it do not, it commends and
sets forth very well unto us the perfection of the
satisfaction that Christ made for us, and the work
of redemption, not only before witness in this
world, but in hell, in that ugsome place ; where
whether He suffered or wrestled with the spirits,
or comforted Abraham, Isaac, and Jacob, I will
not desire to know. If ye like not that which I
have spoken of His suffering, let it go, I will not
strive in it : I will be prejudice to nobody ; weigh
it as ye list. I do but offer it you to consider. It
is like, His soul did somewhat the three days that
His body lay in the grave. To say, He suffered
in hell for us, derogates nothing from His death :
for all things that Christ did before His suffering
on the cross, and after, do work our salvation.
If He had not been incarnate, He had not died :
He was beneficial to us with all things He did.
Christian people should have His suffering for
them in remembrance. Let your gardens monish
you, your pleasant gardens, what Christ suffered
for you in the garden, and what commodity you

have by His suffering. It is His will ye should do so ; He would be had in remembrance. Mix your pleasures with the remembrance of His bitter passion. The whole passion is satisfaction for our sins ; and not the bare death, considering it so nakedly by itself. The manner of speaking of scripture is to be considered. It attributeth our salvation now to one thing, now to another that Christ did ; where indeed it pertained to all.

Our Saviour Christ hath left behind Him a remembrance of His passion, the blessed communion, the celebration of the Lord's Supper : alack ! it hath been long abused, as the sacrifices were before in the old law. The patriarchs used sacrifice in the faith of the Seed of the woman, which should break the serpent's head. The patriarchs sacrificed on hope, and afterward the work was esteemed. There come other after, and they consider not the faith of Abraham and the patriarchs, but do their sacrifice according to their own imagination : even so came it to pass with our blessed communion. In the primitive church, in places when their friends were dead, they used to come together to the holy communion.[1] What!

[1] Bingham, Antiquit. Book xxiii. ch. 3. 12. In the first Prayer Book of Edward VI., the third part of the Burial Service consisted of 'The celebration of the Holy Communion when there is a burial of the dead.' This, though omitted at the revision of the Prayer Book in 1552, was yet incorporated into the Latin Prayer published, chiefly for the use of the Universities and public Schools, in the second year of the reign of Queen Elizabeth. (*Corrie.*)

to remedy them that were dead? No, no, a straw;
it was instituted for no such purpose. But then
they would call to remembrance God's goodness,
and His passion that He suffered for us, wherein
they comforted much their faith.

Others came afterward, and set up all these
kinds of massing, all these kinds of iniquity.
What an abomination is it, the foulest that ever
was, to attribute to man's work our salvation!
God be thanked that we have this blessed communion set forth so now, that we may comfort,
increase, and fortify our faith at that blessed
celebration! If he be guilty of the body of
Christ, that takes it unworthily; he fetcheth great
comfort at it, that eats it worthily. He doth eat
it worthily, that doth eat it in faith. In faith?
in what faith? . . . . It is no bribing judge's or
justice's faith; no rent-raiser's faith; no lease-
monger's faith; nor no seller of benefices' faith;
but the faith in the passion of our Saviour Christ.
We must believe that our Saviour Christ hath
taken us again to His favour, that He hath
delivered us His own body and blood, to plead
with the devil, and by merit of His own passion,
of His own mere liberality. This is the faith, I
tell you, that we must come to the communion
with.

Look where remission of sin is, there is acknow-
ledging of sin also. Faith is a noble duchess, she
hath ever her gentleman-usher going before her,

—the confessing of sins: she hath a train after her,—the fruits of good works, the walking in the commandments of God. He that believeth will not be idle, he will walk; he will do his business. Have ever the gentleman-usher with you. So if ye will try faith, remember this rule,—consider whether the train be waiting upon her. If you have another faith than this, a whoremonger's faith, you are like to go to the scalding-house, and there you shall have two dishes, weeping and gnashing of teeth. Much good do it you! you see your fare. If ye will believe and acknowledge your sins, you shall come to the blessed communion of the bitter passion of Christ worthily, and so attain to everlasting life: to the which the Father of heaven bring you and me! *Amen.*

OUR DAILY BREAD:[1]

St Matthew vi. 11.—'Give us this day our daily bread.'

' Panem nostrum quotidianum da nobis hodie.'

THIS is a very good prayer, if a body should say no more at one time, but that ; for as we see our need, so we shall pray. When we see God's name to be dishonoured, blasphemed and ill spoken of, then a man, a faithful man, should say, 'Our Father, which art in heaven, hallowed be Thy name.' When we see the devil reign, and all the world follow his kingdom, then we may say, 'Our Father, which art in heaven, Thy kingdom come.' When we see that the world followeth her own desires and lusts, and not God's will and His commandments, and it grieveth us to see this, we be sorry for it ; we shall make our moan unto God for it, saying, 'Our Father, which art in heaven, *Fiat voluntas tua*, Thy will be done.' When we lack necessaries for the maintenance of this life, every thing is dear, then we may say, 'Our Father, which art in heaven, give

[1] The fifth of a series of sermons preached by Latimer before the Duchess of Suffolk at Grimsthorpe Castle, Lincolnshire, in 1552.

us this day our daily bread.' Therefore as we see cause, so we should pray. And it is better to say one of these short prayers with a good faith, than the whole psalter without faith.

By this now that I have said, you may perceive that the common opinion and estimation which the people have had of this prayer (the Lord's prayer, I say) is far from that that it is indeed. For it was esteemed for nothing : for when we be disposed to despise a man, and call him an ignorant fool, we say, ' He cannot say his *Paternoster ;* ' and so we made it a light matter, as though every man knew it. But I tell you, it is a great matter ; it containeth weighty things, if it be weighed to the very bottom, as a learned man could do. But as for me, that that I have learned out of the holy scripture and learned men's books, which expound the same, I will shew unto you : but I intend to be short. I have been very long before in the other petitions, which something expound those that follow : therefore I will not tarry so long in them as I have done in the other.

'Give us this day our daily bread.' Every word is to be considered, for they have their importance. This word ' bread ' signifieth all manner of sustenance for the preservation of this life ; all things whereby man should live are contained in this word ' bread.' You must remember what I said by that petition, ' Hallowed be Thy name.' There we pray unto God that He will give us grace to live so that we may, with all our conversations and doings, hallow and sanctify Him, according as His word telleth us. Now forasmuch as the preaching of God's word is most necessary to bring us into this hallowing, we pray in the same petition for the office of preaching. For the sanctifying of the name of God cannot be, except the office of preaching be maintained, and His word be preached and known : therefore in the same petition, when I say, *Sanctificetur*, 'Hallowed be Thy name,' I pray that His word may be spread abroad and known, through which cometh sanctifying. So likewise in this petition, 'Give us this day our daily bread,' we pray for all those things which be necessary and requisite to the sustenance of our souls and bodies.

Now the first and principal thing that we have need of in this life is the magistrates : without a magistrate we should never live well and quietly. Then it is necessary and most needful to pray unto God for them, that the people may have rest, and apply their business, every man in his calling ; the husbandman in tilling and ploughing, the artificer in his business. For you must ever consider, that where war is, there be all discommodities ; no man can do his duty according unto his calling, as appeareth now in Germany, the Emperor and the French king being at

controversy. I warrant you, there is little rest
or quietness. Therefore in this petition we pray
unto God for our magistrates, that they may rule
and govern this realm well and godly; and keep
us from invasions of alienates and strangers; and
to execute justice, and punish malefactors: and
this is so requisite, that we cannot live without it.
Therefore when we say, 'Give us this day our
daily bread;' we pray for the king, his counsellors,
and all his officers.

But not every man that saith these words
understandeth so much; for it is obscurely
included, so that none perceive it but those which
earnestly and diligently consider the same. But
St Paul he expresseth it with more words plainly,
saying, 'I exhort you to make supplications and
prayers for all men, but specially *pro regibus et qui
in sublimitate constituti sunt,* for the kings, and for
those which be aloft.' Whereto? *Ut placidam et
quietam vitam agamus,* 'That we may live godly
and quietly, in all honesty and godliness.'[1] And
when I pray for them, I pray for myself: for I
pray for them that they may rule so, that I and
all men may live quietly and at rest. And to
this end we desire a quiet life, that we may the
better serve God, hear His word, and live after
it. For in the rebels' time, I pray you, what
godliness was shewed amongst them? They
went so far, as it was told, that they defiled other

[1] 1 Tim. ii. 1, 2.

men's wives : what godliness was this? In what estate, think you, were those faithful subjects which at the same time were amongst them? They had sorrow enough, I warrant you. So it appeareth, that where war is, there is right godliness banished and gone. Therefore to pray for a quiet life, that is as much as to pray for a godly life, that we may serve God in our calling, and get our livings uprightly. So it appeareth, that praying for magistrates is as much as to pray for ourselves.

They that be children, and live under the rule of their parents, or have tutors, they pray in this petition for their parents and tutors ; for they be necessary for their bringing up : and God will accept their prayer, as well as theirs which be of age. For God hath no respect of persons ; he is as ready to hear the youngest as the oldest : therefore let them be brought up in godliness, let them know God. Let parents and tutors do their duties to bring them up so, that as soon as their age serveth, they may taste and savour God ; let them fear God in the beginning, and so they shall do also when they be old. Because I speak here of orphans, I shall exhort you to be pitiful unto them ; for it is a thing that pleaseth God, as St James witnesseth, saying, *Religio pura*, &c., ' Pure religion.' [1]

It is a common speech amongst the people,

[1] Jas. i. 27.

and much used, that they say, 'All religious houses [1] are pulled down:' which is a very peevish saying, and not true, for they are not pulled down. That man and that woman that live together godly and quietly, doing the works of their vocation, and fear God, hear His word and keep it; that same is a religious house, that is, that house that pleaseth God. For religion, pure religion, I say, standeth not in wearing of a monk's cowl, but in righteousness, justice, and well-doing, and, as St James saith, in visiting the orphans, and widows that lack their husbands, orphans that lack their parents; to help them when they be poor, to speak for them when they be oppressed: herein standeth true religion, God's religion, I say: the other which was used was an unreligious life, yea, rather an hypocrisy. There is a text in scripture, I never read it but I remember these religious houses: *Estque recta homini via, cujus tamen postremum iter est ad mortem;* 'There is a way, which way seemeth to men to be good, whose end is eternal perdition.' [2] When the end is naught, all is naught. So were these monks' houses, these religious houses. There were many people, specially widows, which would give over house-keeping, and go to such houses, when they might have done much good in maintaining of servants, and relieving of poor

---

[1] *I.e.* Monasteries and nunneries.   [2] Prov. xiv. 13.

people ; but they went their ways. What a madness was that ! Again, how much cause we have to thank God, that we know what is true religion ; that God hath revealed unto us the deceitfulness of those monks, which had a goodly shew before the world of great holiness, but they were naught within. Therefore scripture saith, *Quod excelsum est hominibus, abominabile est coram Deo ;* 'That which is highly esteemed before men is abominable before God.'[1] Therefore that man and woman that live in the fear of God are much better than their houses were.

I read once a story of a holy man, (some say it was St Anthony,) which had been a long season in the wilderness, neither eating nor drinking any thing but bread and water : at the length he thought himself so holy, that there should be nobody like unto him. Therefore he desired of God to know who should be his fellow in heaven. God made him answer, and commanded him to go to Alexandria ; there he should find a cobbler which should be his fellow in heaven. Now he went thither and sought him out, and fell in acquaintance with him, and tarried with him three or four days to see his conversation. In the morning his wife and he prayed together ; then they went to their business, he in his shop, and she about her housewifery. At dinner time they had bread and cheese, wherewith they were

[1] Luke xvi. 15.

well content, and took it thankfully. Their
children were well taught to fear God, and to
say their *Pater-noster*, and the Creed, and the
Ten Commandments; and so he spent his time
in doing his duty truly. I warrant you, he did
not so many false stitches as cobblers do now-a-
days. St Anthony perceiving that, came to
knowledge of himself, and laid away all pride
and presumption. By this ensample you may
learn, that honest conversation and godly living
is much regarded before God; insomuch that this
poor cobbler, doing his duty diligently, was made
St Anthony's fellow. So it appeareth that we be
not destituted of religious houses: those which
apply their business uprightly and hear God's
word, they shall be St Anthony's fellows; that
is to say, they shall be numbered amongst the
children of God.

Further, in this petition the man and wife pray
one for the other. For one is a help unto the
other, and so necessary the one to the other:
therefore they pray one for the other, that God
will spare them their lives, to live together quietly
and godly, according to His ordinance and
institution; and this is good and needful. As
for such as be not married, you shall know that I
do not so much praise marriage, that I should
think that single life is naught; as I have heard
some which will scant allow single life. They
think in their hearts that all those which be not

married be naught : therefore they have a common
saying amongst them, ' What ! ' say they, ' they
be made of such metal as we be made of ; '
thinking them to be naught in their living ; which
suspicions are damnable afore God : for we know
not what gifts God hath given unto them ; therefore we cannot with good conscience condemn
them or judge them.   Truth it is, ' marriage is
good and honourable amongst all men,' as St
Paul witnesseth ;   *Et adulteros et fornicatores
judicabit Dominus*,[1] . . . but not those which live
in single life.   When thou livest in lechery, . . .
then thou shalt be damned : but when thou livest
godly and honestly in single life, it is well and
allowable afore God ; yea, and better than
marriage : for St Paul saith, *Volo vos absque
solicitudine esse*, ' I will have you to be without
carefulness,' that is, unmarried ; and sheweth the
commodities, saying, ' they that be unmarried set
their minds upon God, how to please Him, and
to live after His commandments.   But as for the
other, the man is careful how to please his wife ;
and again, the woman how to please her husband.'[2]
And this is St Paul's saying of the one as well as
of the other.   Therefore I will wish you not to
condemn single life, but take one with the other ;
like as St Paul teacheth us, not to extol the one,
that we should condemn the other.   For St Paul
praiseth as well single life, as marriage ; yea, and

[1] Heb. xiii. 4.   [2] 1 Cor. vii. 32, 34.

L

more too. For those that be single have more
liberties to pray and to serve God than the other :
for they that be married have much trouble and
afflictions in their bodies. This I speak, because
I hear that some there be which condemn single
life. I would have them to know that matrimony
is good, godly, and allowable unto all men: yet for
all that, the single life ought not to be despised or
condemned, seeing that Scripture alloweth it; yea,
and he affirmeth that it is better than matrimony,
if it be clean without sin and offence.

Further, we pray here in this petition for good
servants, that God will send unto us good, faithful,
and trusty servants ; for they are necessary for
this bodily life, that our business may be done :
and those which live in single life have more need
of good trusty servants than those which are
married. Those which are married can better
oversee their servants. For when the man is from
home, at the least the wife overseeth them, and
keepeth them in good order. For I tell you,
servants must be overseen and looked to : if they
be not overseen, what be they ? It is a great gift
of God to have a good servant: for the most part
of servants are but eye-servants ; when their
master is gone, they leave off from their labour,
and play the sluggards : but such servants do
contrary to God's commandment, and shall be
damned in hell for their slothfulness, except they
repent. Therefore, I say, those that be unmarried

have more need of good servants than those which be married; for one of them at the least may always oversee the family. For, as I told you before, the most part of servants be eye-servants; they be nothing when they be not overseen.

There was once a fellow asked a philosopher a question, saying, *Quomodo saginatur equus?* 'How is a horse made fat?' The philosopher made answer, saying, *Oculo domini,* 'With his master's eye.' Not meaning that the horse should be fed with his master's eye, but that the master should oversee the horse, and take heed to the horse-keeper, that the horse might be well fed. For when a man rideth by the way, and cometh to his inn, and giveth unto the hostler his horse to walk, and so he himself sitteth at the table and maketh good cheer, and forgetteth his horse; the hostler cometh and saith, 'Sir, how much bread shall I give unto your horse?' He saith, 'Give him two-penny worth.' I warrant you, this horse shall never be fat. Therefore a man should not say to the hostler, 'Go, give him;' but he should see himself that the horse have it. In like manner, those that have servants must not only command them what they shall do, but they must see that it be done: they must be present, or else it shall never be done.

One other man asked that same philosopher this question, saying, 'What dung is it that maketh a man's land most fruitful in bringing forth much corn?' 'Marry,' said he, *Vestigia domini*, 'The owner's footsteps.' Not meaning that the master should come and walk up and down, and tread the ground ; but he would have him to come and oversee the servants tilling of the ground, commanding them to do it diligently, and so to look himself upon their work : this shall be the best dung, saith the philosopher. Therefore never trust servants, except you may be assured of their diligence ; for I tell you truly, I can come nowhere but I hear masters complaining of their servants. I think verily, they fear not God, they consider not their duties.

Well, I will burthen them with this one text of scripture, and then go forward in my matters. The prophet Jeremy saith,[1] *Maledictus qui facit opus Domini negligenter*. Another translation hath *fraudulenter*, but it is one in effect : 'Cursed be he that doth the work of the Lord negligently or fraudulently,' take which you will. It is no light matter, that God pronounceth them to be cursed. But what is 'cursed?' What is it? 'Cursed' is as much to say as, 'It shall not go well with them ; they shall have no luck ; My face shall be against them.' Is not this a great thing? Truly, consider it as you list, but it is no light matter to be cursed of God, which ruleth heaven and earth. And though the prophet speaketh these words of warriors going to war, yet it may be spoken of all

[1] Jer. xlviii. 10.

servants, yea, of all estates, but specially of servants; for St Paul saith, *Domino Christo servitis :* 'You servants,' saith he, 'you serve the Lord Christ, it is His work.'[1] Then, when it is the Lord's work, take heed how you do it; for cursed is he that doth it negligently. But where is such a servant as Jacob was to Laban? How painful was he! How careful for his master's profit! Insomuch that when somewhat perished, he restored it again of his own. And where is such a servant as Eleazer was to Abraham his master? What a journey had he! How careful he was, and when he came to his journey's end, he would neither eat nor drink afore he had done his master's message; so that all his mind was given only to serve his master, and to do according to his commandments : insomuch that he would neither eat nor drink till he had done according to his master's will! Much like to our Saviour's saying, *Cibus meus est ut faciam voluntatem ejus, qui misit me ;* 'This is My meat, to do the will of Him that sent Me.' I pray you servants, mark this Eleazer well; consider all the circumstances of his diligent and faithful service, and follow it : else if you follow it not, you read it to your own condemnation.

Likewise consider the true service which Joseph, that young man, did unto his master Potiphar, lieutenant of the Tower ; how faithfully

[1] Col. iii. 24.

he served, without any guile or fraud : therefore
God promoted him so, that he was made afterwards the ruler over all Egypt. Likewise consider
how faithful Daniel was in serving king Darius.
Alack, that you servants be stubborn-hearted, and
will not consider this ! You will not remember
that your service is the work of the Lord ; you
will not consider that the curse of God hangeth upon
your heads for your slothfulness and negligence.
Take heed, therefore, and look to your duties.

Now, further : whosoever prayeth this prayer
with a good faithful heart, as he ought to do, he
prayeth for all ploughmen and husbandmen, that
God will prosper and increase their labour ; for
except He give the increase, all their labour and
travail is lost. Therefore it is needful to pray for
them, that God may send His benediction by
their labour ; for without corn and such manner
of sustenance we cannot live. And in that prayer
we include all artificers ; for by their labours God
giveth us many commodities which we could not
lack. We pray also for wholesome air. Item, we
pray for seasonable weather. When we have too
much rain, we pray for fair weather : again, when
we lack rain, we pray that God will send rain.
And in that prayer we pray for our cattle, that
God will preserve them to our use from all
diseases : for without cattle we cannot live ; we
cannot till the ground, nor have meat : therefore
we include them in our prayer too.

So you see that this prayer containeth innumerable things. For we pray for all such things as be expedient and needful for the preservation of this life. And not alone this, but we have here good doctrine and admonition besides. For here we be admonished of the liberality of God our heavenly Father, which He sheweth daily over us. For our Saviour, knowing the liberality of God our heavenly Father, commandeth us to pray. If He would not give us the things we ask, Christ would not have commanded us to pray. If He had borne an ill will against us, Christ would not have sent us to Him. But our Saviour, knowing His liberal heart towards us, commandeth us to pray, and desire all things at His hands.

And here we be admonished of our estate and condition, what we be, namely, beggars. For we ask bread : of whom ? Marry, of God. What are we then ? Marry, beggars : the greatest lords and ladies in England are but beggars afore God. Seeing then that we all are but beggars, why should we then disdain and despise poor men ? Let us therefore consider that we be but beggars ; let us pull down our stomachs. For if we consider the matter well, we are like as they be afore God : for St Paul saith, *Quid habes quod non accepisti ?* 'What hast thou that thou hast not received of God?'[1] Thou art but a beggar, whatsoever thou art : and though there be some

[1] 1 Cor. iv. 7.

very rich, and have great abundance, of whom have they it? Of God. What saith he, that rich man? He saith, 'Our Father, which art in heaven, give us this day our daily bread:' then he is a beggar afore God as well as the poorest man. Further, how continueth the rich man in his riches? Who made him rich? Marry, God. For it is written, *Benedictio Dei facit divitem;* 'The blessing of God maketh rich.'[1] Except God bless, it standeth to no effect: for it is written, *Comedent et non saturabuntur;* 'They shall eat, but yet never be satisfied.'[2] Eat as much as you will, except God feed you, you shall never be full. So likewise, as rich as a man is, yet he cannot augment his riches, nor keep that he hath, except God be with him, except He bless him. Therefore let us not be proud, for we be beggars the best of us.

Note here, that our Saviour biddeth us to say, 'us.' This 'us' lappeth in all other men with my prayer; for every one of us prayeth for another. When I say, 'Give us this day our daily bread,' I pray not for myself only, if I ask as He biddeth me; but I pray for all others. Wherefore say I not, 'Our Father, give me this day my daily bread?' For because God is not my God alone, He is a common God. And here we be admonished to be friendly, loving, and charitable one to another: for what God giveth, I cannot

[1] Prov. x. 22.   [2] Isa. ix. 10.

say, 'This is my own;' but I must say, 'This is ours.' For the rich man cannot say, 'This is mine alone, God hath given it unto me for my own use.' Nor yet hath the poor man any title unto it, to take it away from him. No, the poor man may not do so; for when he doth so, he is a thief afore God and man. But yet the poor man hath title to the rich man's goods; so that the rich man ought to let the poor man have part of his riches to help and to comfort him withal. Therefore when God sendeth unto me much, it is not mine, but ours; it is not given unto me alone, but I must help my poor neighbours withal.

But here I must ask you rich men a question. How chanceth it you have your riches? 'We have them of God,' you will say. But by what means have you them? 'By prayer,' you will say. 'We pray for them unto God, and He giveth us the same.' Very well. But I pray you tell me, what do other men which are not rich? Pray they not as well as you do? 'Yes,' you must say; for you cannot deny it. Then it appeareth that you have your riches not through your own prayers only, but other men help you to pray for them: for they say as well, 'Our Father, give us this day our daily bread,' as you do; and peradventure they be better than you be, and God heareth their prayer sooner than yours. And so it appeareth most manifestly, that you obtain your riches of God, not only through your own prayer, but through other men's too : other men help you to get them at God's hand. Then it followeth, that seeing you get not your riches alone through your own prayer, but through the poor man's prayer, it is meet that the poor man should have part of them ; and you ought to relieve his necessity and poverty.

But what meaneth God by this inequality, that He giveth to some an hundred pound ; unto this man five thousand pound ; unto this man in a manner nothing at all? What meaneth He by this inequality ? Here He meaneth, that the rich ought to distribute his riches abroad amongst the poor : for the rich man is but God's officer, God's treasurer : he ought to distribute them according unto his Lord God's commandment. If every man were rich, then no man would do any thing : therefore God maketh some rich and some poor. Again ; that the rich may have where to exercise his charity, God made some rich and some poor : the poor He sendeth unto the rich to desire of him in God's name help and aid. Therefore, you rich men, when there cometh a poor man unto you, desiring your help, think none otherwise but that God hath sent him unto you ; and remember that thy riches be not thy own, but thou art but a steward over them.

If thou wilt not do it, then cometh in St John, which saith : ' He that hath the substance of this

world, and seeth his brother lack, and helpeth him
not, how remaineth the love of God in him?'[1]
He speaketh not of them that have it not, but of
them that have it : that same man loveth not God,
if he help not his neighbour, having wherewith to
do it. This is a sore and hard word. There be
many which say with their mouth, they love God :
and if a man should ask here this multitude,
whether they love God or no ; they would say,
'Yes, God forbid else!' But if you consider their
unmercifulness unto the poor, you shall see, as St
John said, 'the love of God is not within them.'
Therefore, you rich men, ever consider of whom
you have your riches : be it a thousand pound,
yet you fetch it out of this petition. For this
petition, 'Give us this day our daily bread,' is God's
store-house, God's treasure-house : here lieth all
His provision, and here you fetch it. But ever
have in remembrance that this is a common
prayer : a poor man prayeth as well as thou, and
peradventure God sendeth this riches unto thee
for another man's prayers' sake, which prayeth
for thee, whose prayer is more effectual than thine
own. And therefore you ought to be thankful
unto other men, which pray for you unto God, and
help you to obtain your riches.

Again, this petition is a remedy against this
wicked carefulness of men, when they seek how to
live, and how to get their livings, in such wise,

[1] 1 John iii. 17.

like as if there were no God at all. And then there be some which will not labour as God hath appointed unto them ; but rather give them to falsehood ; to sell false ware, and deceive their neighbours ; or to steal other men's sheep or conies : those fellows are far wide. Let them come to God's treasure-house, that is to say, let them come to God and call upon Him with a good faith, saying, 'Our Father, give us this day our daily bread ;' truly God will hear them. For this is the only remedy that we have here on earth, to come to His treasure-house, and fetch there such things as we lack. Consider this word 'daily.' God promiseth us to feed us daily. If ye believe this, why use you then falsehood and deceit ? Therefore, good people, leave your falsehood ; get you rather to this treasure-house ; then you may be sure of a living : for God hath determined that all that come unto Him, desiring His help, they shall be holpen ; God will not forget them. But our unbelief is so great, we will not come unto Him : we will rather go about to get our living with falsehood, than desire the same of Him.

O what falsehood is used in England, yea, in the whole world ! It were no marvel if the fire from heaven fell upon us, like as it did upon the Sodomites, only for our falsehood's sake ! I will tell you of a false practice that was practised in my country where I dwell. But I will not tell it you to teach you to do the same, but rather to abhor it : for those which use such deceitfulness shall be damned world without end, except they repent. I have known some that had a barren cow : they would fain have had a great deal of money for her ; therefore they go and take a calf of another cow, and put it to this barren cow, and so go to the market, pretending that this cow hath brought that calf ; and so they sell their barren cow six or eight shillings dearer than they should have done else. The man which bought the cow cometh home : peradventure he hath a many of children, and hath no more cattle but this cow, and thinketh he shall have some milk for his children ; but when all things cometh to pass, this is a barren cow, and so this poor man is deceived. The other fellow, which sold the cow, thinketh himself a jolly fellow and a wise merchant ; and he is called one that can make shift for himself.

But I tell thee, whosoever thou art, do so if thou lust, thou shalt do it of this price,—thou shalt go to the devil, and there be hanged on the fiery gallows world without end : and thou art as very a thief as when thou takest a man's purse from him going by the way, and thou sinnest as well against this commandment, *Non facies furtum*, ' Thou shalt do no theft.' But these fellows, commonly, which use such deceitfulness and guiles, can speak so finely, that a man would think butter should scant melt in their mouths.

I tell you one other falsehood. I know that some husbandmen go to the market with a quarter of corn : now they would fain sell dear the worst as well as the best ; therefore they use this policy : they go and put a strike [1] of fine malt or corn in the bottom of the sack, then they put two strikes of the worst they had ; then a good strike aloft in the sack's mouth, and so they come to the market. Now there cometh a buyer, asking, ' Sir, is this good malt ? ' ' I warrant you,' saith he, ' there is no better in this town.' And so he selleth all his malt or corn for the best, when there be but two strikes of the best in his sack. The man that buyeth it thinketh he hath good malt, he cometh home ; when he putteth the malt out of the sack, the strike which was in the bottom covereth the ill malt which was in the midst ; and so the good man shall never perceive the fraud till he cometh to the occupying of the corn. The other man that sold it taketh this for a policy : but it is theft afore God, and he is bound to make restitution of so much as those two strikes which were naught were sold too dear ; so much he ought to restore, or else he shall never come to heaven, if God be true in His Word.

I could tell you of one other falsehood, how they make wool to weigh much ; but I will not tell it you. If you learn to do those falsehoods whereof I have told you now, then take the sauce

[1] A bushel,

with it, namely, that you shall never see the bliss
of heaven, but be damned world without end,
with the devil and all his angels. Now go when
it please you, use falsehood. But I pray you,
wherefore will you deceive your neighbour, whom
you ought to love as well as your own self? Consider the matter, good people, what a dangerous
thing it is to fall into the hands of the ever-living God.
Leave falsehood; abhor it. Be true and faithful
in your calling. *Quærite regnum Dei, et justitiam
ejus, et cetera omnia adjicientur vobis :* 'Seek the
kingdom of God, and the righteousness thereof,
then all things necessary for you shall come unto
you unlooked for.' [1]

Therefore in this petition note first God's goodness, how gentle He is towards us; insomuch that
He would have us to come unto Him and take of
Him all things. Then again, note what we be,
namely, beggars, for we beg of Him; which admonisheth us to leave stoutness and proudness, and to be
humble. Note what is 'our;' namely, that one
prayeth for another, and that this storehouse
is common unto all men. Note again, what we
be when we be false;—the children of the devil
and enemies unto God.

There be some men which would have this
petition not to import or contain these bodily
things as things which be too vile to be desired at
God's hand; therefore they expound it altogether

[1] Matt. vi. 33.

spiritually, of things pertaining unto the soul only ;
which opinion, truly, I do not greatly like. For
shall I trust God for my soul, and shall I not
trust Him for my body ? Therefore I take it,
that all things necessary to soul and body are
contained in this petition ; and we ought to seek
all things necessary to our bodily food only in this
storehouse.

But you must not take my sayings after such
sort, as though you should do nothing but sit and
pray ; and yet you should have your dinner and
supper made ready for you. No, not so : but you
must labour, you must do the work of your
vocation. *Quærite regnum Dei*, 'Seek the kingdom of heaven : ' you must set those two things
together, works and prayer. He that is true in
his vocation, doing according as God willeth him
to do, and then prayeth unto God, that man or
woman may be assured of their living ; as sure,
I say, as God is God. As for the wicked, indeed
God of His exceeding mercy and liberality findeth
them ; and sometimes they fare better than the
good man doth : but for all that the wicked man hath
ever an ill conscience ; he doth wrong unto God ;
he is an usurper, he hath no right unto it. The
good and godly man he hath right unto it ; for
he cometh by it lawfully, by his prayer and travail.
But these covetous men, think ye, say they this
prayer with a faithful heart, ' Our Father, which
art in heaven ; Give us this day our daily bread ? '

Think ye they say it from the bottom of their hearts? No, no; they do but mock God, they laugh Him to scorn, when they say these words. For they have their bread, their silver and gold in their coffers, in their chests, in their bags or budgets; therefore they have no savour of God: else they would shew themselves liberal unto their poor neighbours; they would open their chests and bags, and lay out and help their brethren in Christ. They be as yet but scorners: they say this prayer like as the Turk might say it.

Consider this word, 'Give.' Certainly, we must labour, yet we must not so magnify our labour as though we gat our living by it. For labour as long as thou wilt, thou shalt have no profit by it, except the Lord increase thy labour. Therefore we must thank Him for it; He doth it; He giveth it. To whom? *Laboranti et poscenti*, 'Unto him that laboureth and prayeth.' That man that is so disposed shall not lack, as He saith, *Dabit Spiritum Sanctum poscentibus illum;* 'He will give the Holy Ghost unto them that desire the same.' [1] Then, we must ask; for He giveth not to sluggards. Indeed, they have His benefits; they live wealthily: but, as I told you afore, they have it with an ill conscience, not lawfully. Therefore Christ saith, *Solem suum oriri sinit super justos et injustos;* 'He suffers His sun to rise upon the just and unjust.' [2] Also, *Nemo scit an odio vel*

[1] Luke vi. 13.   [2] Matt. v. 45.

M

amore sit dignus ; ' We cannot tell outwardly by these worldly things, which be in the favour of God, and which be not ; '[1] for they be common unto good and bad : but the wicked have it not with a good conscience ; the upright, good man hath his living through his labour and faithful prayer. Beware that you trust not in your labour, as though you got your living by it : for, as St Paul saith, *Qui plantat nihil est, neque qui rigat, sed qui dat incrementum Deus ;* ' Neither he that planteth is aught, nor he that watereth, but God that giveth the increase.'[2] Except God give the increase, all our labour is lost. They that be the children of this world, as covetous persons, extortioners, oppressors, caterpillars, usurers, think you they come to God's storehouse ? No, no, they do not ; they have not the understanding of it ; they cannot tell what it meaneth. For they look not to get their livings at God's storehouse, but rather they think to get it with deceit and falsehood, with oppression, and wrong doings. For they think that all things be lawful unto them ; therefore they think that though they take other men's goods through subtlety and crafts, it is no sin. But I tell you, those things which we buy, or get with our labour, or are given us by inheritance, or other ways, those things be ours by the law ; which maketh *meum* and *tuum*, mine and thine. Now all things gotten otherwise are not ours ; as

---

[1] Eccles. ix. 1. [2] 1 Cor. iii. 7.

those things which be gotten by crafty convey-
ances, by guile and fraud, by robbery and stealing,
by extortion and oppression, by hand-making, or
howsoever you come by it beside the right way, it
is not yours ; insomuch that you may not give it
for God's sake, for God hateth it.

But you will say, ' What shall we do with the
good gotten by unlawful means ? ' Marry, I tell
thee : make restitution ; which is the only way
that pleaseth God. O Lord, what bribery, falsehood, deceiving, false getting of goods is in
England ! And yet for all that, we hear nothing
of restitution ; which is a miserable thing. I tell
you, none of them which have taken their neighbour's goods from him by any manner of falsehood, none of them, I say, shall be saved, except
they make restitution, either in affect or effect ;
in effect, when they be able ; in affect, when they
be not able in no wise. Ezekiel saith, *Si impius
egerit pœnitentiam, et rapinam reddiderit ;* ' When
the ungodly doth repent, and restoreth the goods
gotten wrongfully and unlawfully.' [1] For unlawful
goods ought to be restored again : without restitution look not for salvation. Also, this is a true
sentence used of St Augustine, *Non remittetur
peccatum, nisi restituatur ablatum ;* ' Robbery,
falsehood, or otherwise ill-gotten goods, cannot be
forgiven of God, except it be restored again.'
Zacheus, that good publican, that common officer,

[1] Ez. xviii. 27.

he gave a good ensample unto all bribers and
extortioners. I would they all would follow his
ensample! He exercised not open robbery ; he
killed no man by the way ; but with crafts and
subtilties he deceived the poor. When the poor
men came to him, he bade them to come again
another day ; and so delayed the time, till at the
length he wearied poor men, and so gat somewhat
of them. Such fellows are now, in our time, very
good cheap ; but they will not learn the second
lesson. They have read the first lesson, how
Zachee was a bribe-taker ; but they will not read
the second: they say A, but they will not say B.
What is the second lesson ? *Si quem defraudavi,
reddam quadruplum;* 'If I have deceived any
man, I will restore it fourfold.'[1] But we may
argue that they be not such fellows as Zacheus
was, for we hear nothing of restitution ; they lack
right repentance.

It is a wonderful thing to see, that Christian
people will live in such an estate, wherein they
know themselves to be damned : for when they
go to bed, they go in the name of the devil.
Finally, whatsoever they do, they do it in his
name, because they be out of the favour of God.
God loveth them not ; therefore, I say, it is to be
lamented that we hear nothing of restitution. St
Paul saith, *Qui furabatur non amplius furetur;*
'He that stale, let him steal no more.'[2] Which

---

[1] Luke xix. 8. [2] Eph. iv. 28.

words teach us, that he which hath stolen or deceived, and keepeth it, he is a strong thief so long till he restore again the thing taken ; and shall look for no remission of his sins at God's hand, till he hath restored again such goods.

There be some which say, ' Repentance or contrition will serve ; it is enough when I am sorry for it.'

Those fellows cannot tell what repentance meaneth. Look upon Zacheus : he did repent, but restitution by and by followed. So let us do too : let us live uprightly and godly ; and when we have done amiss, or deceived anybody, let us make restitution. And after, beware of such sins, of such deceitfulness ; but rather let us call upon God, and resort to His storehouse, and labour faithfully and truly for our livings. Whosoever is so disposed, him God will favour, and he shall lack nothing : as for the other impenitent sluggards, they be devourers and usurpers of God's gifts, and therefore shall be punished, world without end, in everlasting fire.

Remember this word ' our : ' what it meaneth I told you. And here I have occasion to speak of the proprieties of things : for I fear, if I should leave it so, some of you would report me wrongfully, and affirm, that all things should be common. I say not so. Certain it is, that God hath ordained proprieties of things, so that that which is mine is not thine ; and what thou hast I cannot take from thee. If all things were common, there could be no theft, and so this commandment, *Non facies furtum*, 'Thou shalt not steal,' were in vain. But it is not so: the laws of the realm make *meum et tuum*, mine and thine. If I have things by those laws, then I have them well. But this you must not forget, that St Paul saith, *Sitis necessitatibus sanctorum communicantes;* 'Relieve the necessity of those which have need.'   Things are not so common, that another man may take my goods from me, for this is theft ; but they are so common, that we ought to distribute them unto the poor, to help them, and to comfort them with it.   We ought one to help another ; for this is a standing sentence : *Qui habuerit substantiam hujus mundi, et viderit fratrem suum necessitatem habere, et clauserit viscera sua ab eo, quomodo caritas Dei manet in eo ?* [1] 'He that hath the substance of this world, and shall see his brother to have need, and shutteth up his entire affection from him, how dwelleth the love of God in him ?'

There was a certain manner of having things in common in the time of the apostles. For some good men, as Barnabas was, sold their lands and possessions, and brought the money unto the apostles : but that was done for this cause,—there was a great many of Christian people at that time entreated very ill, insomuch that they left all their goods : now, such folk came unto the apostles for

[1] 1 John iii. 17.

aid and help ; therefore those which were faithful
men, seeing the poverty of their brethren, went
and sold that that they had, and spent the money
amongst such poor which were newly made
Christians.   Amongst others which sold their
goods there was one Ananias and Saphira his
wife, two very subtile persons : they went and
sold their goods too ; but they played a wise
part : they would not stand in danger of the
losing of all their goods ; therefore they agreed
together, and took the one part from the money,
and laid it up ; with the other part they came to
Peter, affirming that to be the whole money.

For they thought in their hearts, like as all
unfaithful men do, 'We cannot tell how long
this religion shall abide ; it is good to be wise,
and keep somewhat in store, whatsoever shall
happen.'

Now Peter, knowing by the Holy Ghost their
falsehood, first slew him with one word, and after
her too : which indeed is a fearful ensample,
whereby we should be monished to beware of lies
and falsehood.   For though God punish thee not
by and by, as He did this Ananias, yet He shall
find thee ; surely He will not forget thee.   Therefore learn here to take heed of falsehood, and
beware of lies.   For this Ananias, this wilful
Ananias, I say, because of this wilful lie, went to
hell with his wife, and there shall be punished
world without end.   Where you see what a thing

it is to make a lie. This Ananias needed not to
sell his lands, he had no such commandment :
but seeing he did so, and then came and brought
but half the price, making a pretence as though
he had brought all, for that he was punished so
grievously.   O what lies are made now-a-days in
England, here and there in the markets ! truly it
is a pitiful thing that we nothing consider it.
This one ensample of Ananias and Saphira, their
punishment, is able to condemn the whole world.

You have heard now, how men had things in
common in the first church : but St Paul he
teacheth us how things ought to be in common
amongst us, saying, *Sitis necessitatibus sanctorum
communicantes ;* ‘Help the necessity of those
which be poor.’ Our good is not so ours that
we may do with it what us listeth ; but we ought
to distribute it unto them which have need.   No
man, as I told you before, ought to take away
my goods from me ; but I ought to distribute
that that I may spare, and help the poor withal.
Communicantes necessitatibus, saith St Paul ; ‘Distribute them unto the poor,’ let them lack nothing ;
but help them with such things as you may spare.
For so it is written, *Cui plus datum est, plus re-
quiretur ab illo ;* ‘He that hath much, must make
account for much ; and if he have not spent it
well, he must make the heavier account.’   But
I speak not this to let poor folks from labour ;
for we must labour and do the works of our

vocation, every one in his calling: for so it is written, *Labores manuum tuarum manducabis, et bene tibi erit,* 'Thou shalt eat thy hand-labour, and it shall go well with thee.' That is to say, every man shall work for his living, and shall not be a sluggard, as a great many be: every man shall labour and pray; then God will send him his living. St Paul saith, *Qui non laborat, non comedat;* 'He that laboureth not, let him not eat.'[1] Therefore those lubbers which will not labour, and might labour, it is a good thing to punish them according unto the king's most godly statutes. For God Himself saith, *In sudore vultus tui vesceris pane tuo;* 'In the sweat of thy face thou shalt eat thy bread.'[2] Then cometh in St Paul, who saith, *Magis autem laboret, ut det indigentibus;* 'Let him labour the sorer, that he may have wherewith to help the poor.'[3] And Christ Himself saith, *Melius est dare quam accipere;* 'It is better to give than to take.'[4] So Christ, and all His apostles, yea, the whole scripture admonisheth us ever of our neighbour, to take heed of Him, to be pitiful unto Him: but God knoweth there be a great many which care little for their neighbours. They do like as Cain did, when God asked him, 'Cain, where is thy brother Abel?' 'What,' saith he, 'am I my brother's keeper?'[5]

---

[1] 2 Thess. iii. 10.　　　[2] Gen. iii. 19.
[3] Ephes. iv. 28.　　　[4] Acts xx. 35.
[5] Gen. iv. 9.

So these rich franklings,[1] these covetous
fellows, they scrape all to themselves, they
think they should care for nobody else but for
themselves : God commandeth the poor man
to labour the sorer, to the end that he may be
able to help his poor neighbour : how much more
ought the rich to be liberal unto them !

But you will say, 'Here is a marvellous doctrine,
which commandeth nothing but "Give, Give : " if
I shall follow this doctrine, I shall give so much,
that at the length I shall have nothing left for
myself.' These be words of infidelity ; he that
speaketh such words is a faithless man. And I
pray you, tell me, have ye heard of any man
that came to poverty, because he gave unto the
poor ? Have you heard tell of such a one ? No,
I am sure you have not. And I dare lay my
head to pledge for it, that no man living hath
come, or shall hereafter come to poverty, because
he hath been liberal in helping the poor. For
God is a true God, and no liar : He promiseth
us in His word, that we shall have the more by
giving to the needy. Therefore the way to get
is to scatter that that you have. Give, and you
shall gain. If you ask me, 'How shall I get
riches ? ' I make thee this answer : 'Scatter
that that thou hast ; for giving is gaining.' But
you must take heed, and scatter it according unto
God's will and pleasure ; that is, to relieve the

---

[1] A man above a vassal ; a freeholder.

poor withal, to scatter it amongst the flock of Christ. Whosoever giveth so shall surely gain : for Christ saith, *Date et dabitur vobis ;* 'Give, and it shall be given unto you.'[1] *Dabitur*, 'it shall be given unto you.' This is a sweet word, we can well away with that ; but how shall we come by it ? *Date*, 'Give.' This is the way to get, to relieve the poor.

Therefore this is a false and wicked proposition, to think that with giving unto the poor we shall come to poverty. What a giver was Loth, that good man : came he to poverty through giving ? No, no ; he was a great rich man. Abraham, the father of all believers, what a liberal man was he ; insomuch that he sat by his door watching when anybody went by the way, that he might call him, and relieve his necessity ! What, came he to poverty ? No, no : he died a great rich man. Therefore let us follow the ensample of Loth and Abraham : let us be liberal, and then we shall augment our stock. For this is a most certain and true word, *Date, et dabitur vobis ;* 'Give, and it shall be given unto you.'

But we believe it not ; we cannot away with it. The most part of us are more given to take from the poor, than to relieve their poverty. They be so careful for their children, that they cannot tell when they be well. They purchase this house and that house ; but what saith the prophet ?

[1] Luke vi. 38.

Væ, qui conjungitis domum domui; ' Woe be unto
you that join house to house ! ' [1] the curse of God
hangeth over your heads. Christ saith, *Qui diligit
patrem vel matrem vel filios plus quam me non est
me dignus;* ' He that loveth his father or mother
or children more than Me, he is not meet for Me.' [2]
Therefore those which scrape and gather ever for
their children, and in the mean season forget the
poor, whom God would have relieved ; those, I
say, regard their children more than God's commandments : for their children must be set up,
and the poor miserable people is forgotten in the
mean season. There is a common saying amongst
the worldlings, Happy is that child whose father
goeth to the devil : but this is a worldly happiness.
The same is seen when the child can begin with
two hundred pound, whereas his father began with
nothing : it is a wicked happiness, if the father gat
those goods wickedly. And there is no doubt but
many a father goeth to the devil for his child's
sake ; in that he neglected God's commandment,
scraped for his child, and forgat to relieve his poor
miserable neighbour. We have in scripture, *Qui
miseretur pauperis, fœneratur Deo;* ' Whosoever
hath pity over the poor, he lendeth unto God
upon usury : ' [3] that is to say, God will give it
unto him again with increase : this is a lawful and
godly usury.

Certain it is, that usury was allowed by the

[1] Isa. v. 8.   [2] Matt. x. 37.   [3] Prov. xix. 17.

laws of this realm ; yet it followed not that usury
was godly, nor allowed before God. For it is not
a good argument, to say, ' It is forbidden to take
ten pounds of the hundred, *ergo*, I may take five : '
like as a thief cannot say, ' It is forbidden in the
law to steal thirteen-pence half-penny ; *ergo*, I may
steal six-pence, or three-pence, or two-pence.' No,
no ; this reasoning will not serve afore God : for
though the law of this realm hangeth him not, if
he steal four-pence, yet for all that he is a thief
before God, and shall be hanged on the fiery
gallows in hell. So he that occupieth usury,
though by the laws of this realm he might do
it without punishment, (for the laws are not so
precise,) yet for all that he doth wickedly in the
sight of God. For usury is wicked before God,
be it small or great ; like as theft is wicked.

But I will tell you how you shall be usurers to
get much gain. Give it unto the poor ; then God
will give it to thee with gain. Give twenty pence,
and thou shalt have forty pence. It shall come
again, thou shalt not lose it ; or else God is not
God. What needeth it to use such deceitfulness
and falsehood to get riches ? Take a lawful way
to get them ; that is, to scatter this abroad that
thou hast, and then thou shalt have it again with
great gain : *quadruplum*, 'four times,' saith scripture.
Now God's word saith, that I shall have again
that which I laid out with usury, with gain. Is
it true that God saith ? Yes ; then let me not

think, that giving unto the poor doth diminish my
stock, when God saith the contrary, namely, that
it shall increase; or else we make God a liar.
For if I believe not His sayings, then by mine
infidelity I make Him a liar, as much as is in me.
Therefore learn here to commit usury: and specially
you rich men, you must learn this lesson well; for
of you it is written, 'Whosoever hath much, must
make account of much.' And you have much,
not to that end, to do with it what you lust; but
you must spend it as God appointeth you in His
word to do: for no rich man can say before God,
'This is my own.' No, he is but an officer over
it, an almoner, God's treasurer.

Our Saviour saith, *Omnis qui reliquerit agrum,*
&c., centuplum accipiet; 'Whosoever shall leave
his field, shall receive it again an hundred fold.'[1]
As, if I should be examined now of the papists, if
they should ask me, 'Believe you in the mass?'
I say, 'No; according unto God's Word, and my
conscience, it is naught, it is but deceitfulness, it
is the devil's doctrine.' Now I must go to prison,
I leave all things behind me, wife and children,
goods and land, and all my friends: I leave them
for Christ's sake, in His quarrel. What saith our
Saviour unto it? *Centuplum accipiet;* 'I shall
have a hundred times so much.' Now though
this be spoken in such wise, yet it may be understood of alms-giving too. For that man or woman

[1] Mark x. 29.

that can find in their hearts for God's sake to leave ten shillings or ten pounds, they shall have ' an hundred-fold again in this life, and in the world to come life everlasting.' If this will not move our hearts, then they are more than stony and flinty ; then our damnation is just and well deserved. For to give alms, it is like as when a man cometh unto me, and desireth an empty purse of me : I lend him the purse, he cometh by and by and bringeth it full of money, and giveth it me ; so that I have now my purse again, and the money too. So it is to give alms : we lend an empty purse, and take a full purse for it. Therefore let us persuade ourselves in our hearts, that to give for God's sake is no loss unto us, but great gain. And truly the poor man doth more for the rich man in taking things of him, than the rich doth for the poor in giving them. For the rich giveth but only worldly goods, but the poor giveth him by the promise of God all felicity.

Quotidianum, ' Daily.' Here we learn to cast away all carefulness, and to come to this store-house of God, where we shall have all things competent both for our souls and bodies. Further, in this petition we desire that God will feed not only our bodies, but also our souls ; and so we pray for the office of preaching. For like as the body must be fed daily with meat, so the soul requireth her meat, which is the word of God. Therefore we pray here for all the clergy, that they may do their duties, and feed us with the word of God according to their calling.

Now I have troubled you long, therefore I will make an end. I desire you remember to resort to this storehouse : whatsoever ye have need of, come hither ; here are all things necessary for your soul and body, only desire them. But you have heard how you must be apparelled ; you must labour and do your duties, and then come, and you shall find all things necessary for you : and specially now at this time let us resort unto God ; for it is a great drought, as we think, and we had need of rain. Let us therefore resort unto our loving Father, which promiseth, that when we call upon Him with a faithful heart, He will hear us. Let us therefore desire Him to rule the matter so, that we may have our bodily sustenance. We have the ensample of Elias, whose prayer God heard. Therefore let us pray this prayer, which our Saviour and Redeemer Jesus Christ Himself taught us, saying, 'Our Father, which art in heaven,' &c. *Amen.*

THE END.